THE QUANDARY

Feeling Responsible for What's Not Mine

Foreword by Pastor Antonio M. Matthews
Sarita Lynn

Copyright © 2017 by Sarita Lynn

All rights reserved. No part of this publication may be reproduced, photocopied. stored in a retrieval system or transmitted in any form or by any means-for example, electronic, photocopy, audio recording-without the prior written permission of the publisher.

Paperback ISBN:978-0-9987653-2-7

eBook ISBN: 978-0-9987653-1-0

Printed in the United States of America

Copyright case number 1-4612533691

www.skiepublishing.com

www.skiepublishing@gmail.com

Published by:

Foreword

By Pastor Antonio M. Matthews

The wonderful, admirable, yet sometimes frustrating gift of life and the process, the playing out, or the unfolding of it can oftentimes leave us in a state of perpetual perplexity. To do or *not* to do. "To be or not to be" (Shakespeare). To go or *not* to go. To become or *not* to become. To *love* or *not* to love. These are all questions we are faced with in the process of life, questions that must be decided upon with answers that can either further complicate life or produce moments of growth, forever seared into the recesses of our minds. To love or NOT to love is a life- altering decision in and of itself. The choice of love has so many variables and nuances, most of the time without the consideration of the one doing the loving. In life, everyone wants to love, and everyone wants to be loved. Often the one loving will go to great lengths to be loved, feel loved, and experience love until his or her actions overcompensate. Encountering reciprocity for the love given while coming to a revelation that what's being received from those we love is only pacification to continue the outpouring of the love being given—that's when loving the other person becomes death to you. That's when loving the other person becomes work and a chore. That's when loving becomes a quandary!

Love makes you vulnerable. Your heart is exposed. The nature of your being is highlighted. People see who you really are when you are fully engrossed in loving them. When people receive your love, but don't possess the heart of the one giving it, you are being used and taken for granted. However, the person giving the love desires so much to be accepted and appreciated and has such a great longing for the same, he or she will continue to love on empty for just a sample of the authentic. So, we give just to feel liked, and we give to feel needed. All the while, we are killing two people—the one loving and the one being loved. Now we are giving without the essence of better judgement. Even when we know it could hurt us, we want the other person to like us. We sometimes ignore the consequences. Herein lies the quandary! Here lie the questions, what do I do when loving you has become a responsibility that's not necessarily mine to own? How do I handle it when my heart is genuine in loving but enabling in deed?

I'm glad you asked those questions because my Spiritual Daughter Sarita Lynn has penned the perfect book to answer the tough, hard-to-ask, and hard-to-address questions. If the authenticity of your love has turned into enabling, you *need* this book! If life has left you in quandaries and places where decisions need to be made, Sarita Lynn tells you how to make them. She teaches how to endure the consequences that come from making that decision. If you have dealt with family realities that have stunted your development and success and you need to turn those tragedies into triumphs, then read this book. I've read it; now I recommend it!

Pastor Antonio M. Matthews
Senior Pastor/Teacher
Tabernacle of Praise Church Waldorf, MD

Dedication

This book is dedicated to my late brother, George Patrick Turner, who died prematurely at the age of forty-two of a drug overdose. My mind replays the reality of my involvement in enabling George for years, and ultimately in his death, that I want to forget. I miss him so much. Not a day goes by that I don't wish he were here with me or I that could pick up the phone to call. Every time I speak to his daughter, Kaylah, I'm reminded of him. You have left me a piece of you, George. You will forever be in my heart. For all the times, I said yes when I should have said no, I'm able to write this book.

George and I were only thirteen months apart in age. We were inseparable growing up. I was one of those typical sisters who thought I was his mother and sister. I would tell him what, when, and how to do things, then state why my decision was best. When George was born, my mother told me, "That's your baby, Sarita," just so I wouldn't get jealous. It was then my days of being an enabler began.

To anyone who has had to struggle to survive, this book is dedicated to you. Writing this book would not have been possible if it hadn't been for God. He protected me through my foolish decisions, and then gave me the strength to speak about the journey. To the countless people, I've enabled in hopes of meeting their needs and covering my insecurities, I share my experiences. I pray that the story I'm about to share makes a difference in someone's life. Rest in Peace, George.

TABLE OF CONTENTS

Dedication	6
Introduction	9
I'll Do It	15
Support vs. Enabling	29
Wanting More for You	43
Truth or Manipulation	67
Trusting the Process	77
When Enough Is Enough	93
Moving Past the Pain and Forgiving	105
Making Me a Priority	119
Conclusion	127
Intercession for Results	128
Take It to the Word	135
Resources	141
About the Author	143

INTRODUCTION

This book was birthed from a desire to be everything to everyone while depleting myself. Somehow my decisions led me to gravitate to the neediest of people in hopes of rescuing and fixing them while masking my own internal voids. I didn't like to see anyone lacking or hurting, so I took it upon myself to insert my abilities to circumvent his or her learning experience. I've always had a big heart with no boundaries. When I love, I love hard. Loving carelessly led me down many roads of repeated disappointments. How many of you know that loving without boundaries or limitations can set you up for a catastrophic collision? I didn't fully grasp how all my yeses would lead me down a path of pain, frustration, and resentment. I had to eventually learn that my current state was only a mirror of the years of my decision-making and words I'd spoken. No one did it to me, but me. As an enabler, it's easy to be in a *quandary*, feeling responsible for what's not mine.

Sometimes when a person has an inner compulsion to be needed and accepted she/he makes decisions out of her/his emotions, instead of intellect. No one is an enabler just for the sake of it. It's a disease just like alcoholism and drug addiction. It's an emotional impulse to hear a need and go out of your way to fix it without weighing the consequences. When your life is out of balance, you live for that moment. Living for the moment doesn't allow you to see the bigger picture, or consider the cost of your time, mental state, finances, relationships, or health. Suddenly, you commit to doing something that you really didn't want to do in the first place. Then you ask yourself, *Why did I just agree to do that?* Then it's too late; you are a person of your word, and pride will not allow you to back out now.

Because of your indecisiveness, your choices constantly change. You begin to obsess over minute things, such as, *I shouldn't have responded like that in the e-mail. They're probably going to think I'm mad. Should I apologize although they were wrong?* Doubt after doubt.

You have a story to tell, and maybe your experience is slightly different from mine. You can gain strength from learning

INTRODUCTION

from someone else's struggle. Gaining wisdom doesn't have to always come from your own mistakes. You can learn from someone else's experience and avoid the heartache and pitfalls.

If I could talk to my younger self, I would say, "Sarita, lighten up on yourself. Don't put so much emphasis on what others think of you, and just do your best." Over the years, I've had to learn to stop putting unrealistic expectations on myself. While I put a lot of emphasis on maintaining the shell of who I am, I didn't invest nearly as much in the inner core of my happiness.

Just know that what you see is not always what you get. When you observe someone, how deep are you willing to look to see who they are? Many people like to keep their realities confined out of fear of becoming a victim of their own circumstances. To get to know someone takes time and an openness to accept what you see. The outer circumference is only a miniscule reflection of a person's existence. There's more than meets the eye.

As I think over my life, I've endured a lot of traumatic events that could have caused me to give up on life. I've endured an alcoholic father as a child, an abusive relationship, unemployment, my father dying of colon cancer, my brother dying of a drug overdose, divorce, and foreclosure. Through all of that, something within me

THE QUANDARY

would never allow me to stop pressing through the pain. I always knew something great was just waiting for me around the corner. People always looked at me and thought I had it all together. I appeared strong and confident, and according to my external appearance, I had it all together. Little did they know that internally, I was in pain, crying out for help; for someone to rescue me.

I used all types of coping mechanisms to survive, and to cover my inadequacies and vulnerabilities. For many seasons, I wore the masks of enablement, makeup, alcohol, people-pleasing, and control. I used these disguises to cope with circumstances, relationships, and life. When I didn't want to focus on me, I would focus on enabling someone else. Codependent relationships are a type of dysfunctional relationship where one person supports or enables another person's addiction, poor mental health, immaturity, irresponsibility, or under-achievement. It's always easier to look at someone else's needs or shortcomings instead of your own. To look internally required me to dissect why I acted the way I did, and then come up with a strategy to make changes. I wasn't ready for true transparency. My disguises helped me to camouflage what I didn't want others to see in me. They helped me to hold on a little longer until I was strong enough to deal with my own truths. One thing I know for sure is that

INTRODUCTION

there was a purpose and benefit to hiding behind my masks. Some people would tell you that wearing a mask is inauthentic, but I believe I obtained some benefits from wearing mine. Thanks to those masks, I could temporarily cope; persevere. I've seen many people end their own lives because they couldn't cope with adversity

Webster defines a face mask is a protective covering. Women should apply a facial mask monthly for an extended period to exfoliate dead skin particles. It is only after the mask is removed and the skin is exposed that you have a more vibrant look and feel about yourself. You begin to exude radiance. So, if you've worn a mask at any point in your life just know it served a purpose.

THE QUANDARY

CHAPTER *One*
I'll Do It

Those who are typically accused of being controlling are waiting for someone else to take the lead. On April 7, 2013, it started off as a typical day at work until I received a call from my mother stating that she received a call informing her George was deceased. A million questions rushed through my mind, along with an overwhelming feeling of a void, helplessness, and anger. I immediately jumped in my car and left work not knowing which direction to go first. My faith was strong, and I was hoping it was all a hoax; George would call my mom or be home by the time I got there.

As I drove down the street, my mind continued to race. Where is my brother? Where should we start to look for him? Is he dead or alive? Should I call the local hospitals, police precincts, or elsewhere? I couldn't cry yet because there were decisions that needed to be made, and I needed to control my emotions and maintain a level head. I had to be strong for my mother. I had learned to process bad news as a business decision, and deal with my emotions later. I'm not saying it's the best method, but it's what I've always done. My only goal was to find George, still wondering if he was dead or alive.

What do I do with this information I just received? I didn't know if I should scream, cry, or chalk it up as a hoax. I thought, *if this rumor is true, how could such sensitive information be relayed so frivolously?* No compassion, no visit to the family home to make sure it was received with sympathy; just a phone call. How could this be true? I had hopes and dreams for George's future. He couldn't die on me; Dad had just died a few years prior.

Growing up, my siblings and I couldn't have been any less alike if we had been strangers. I would ask myself, *How did Felicia, George, and I grow up in the same house and have very little in common?* Felicia was the oldest sibling, I was the middle child, and George was the youngest. Something about those baby boys gives you enough material to write a book. Felicia and I were four years apart in age, and weren't very close growing up. With Felicia being the oldest sibling, she had more responsibilities around the house, because our parents had to work. I was the annoying little sister around whom she didn't want to hang. That left George and me, who were thick as thieves. We were only thirteen months apart, and we did everything together. As the baby boy, he was spoiled by my mom and me. He was my brother, son, and best friend. I would laugh at anything George would say. I was always in trouble with my dad for laughing at the dinner table and goofing around. George would look at me, and I would burst out with laughter.

My brother was a fun-loving kid but always pushed the envelope. As a youngster, he decided to play with matches in his room one day. The bed caught on fire, and he ran out of the house in fear of getting in trouble. Suddenly the house was engulfed in smoke. My dad went running upstairs to look for George and wouldn't leave until he found him. It took numerous firefighters to pull my dad out of the house, because he didn't want to leave his son. We had to spend the rest of the summer in the country with our grandparents while the house was being renovated. This worked out for our parents because we were sent to the South every summer thereafter.

Under our roof, there was division amongst the siblings of where we belonged, so we built alliances with whom we felt most accepted. Felicia was always a daddy's girl, so George and I gravitated toward my mom. It made me wonder what happened from the time my dad fought through the fire to look for George to getting to the feelings of isolation that George and I experienced. This discord resulted in many years of searching for the approval of the other parent.

Millions of people go their entire lives seeking someone's approval that they may never receive. This feeling resulted in me questioning my self-worth and ability to receive love. Why wasn't I good enough, and what did I do wrong? I learned at an early age my answer to what I thought was the burning question, "How do I get what I need from someone who isn't willing to freely give it to me?" I started to enable!

I enabled my dad for his love and attention, so I would do anything that brought about acceptance and approval. I enabled my mom as a small child, because I felt she didn't protect herself when she needed to. She didn't take up for herself or have a voice for right or wrong, so I would speak up for her. When she was going through something emotional, I would encourage her and let her know she deserved better. I thank God for keeping His hand on me, because I could have been gone a long time ago. Since my dad liked to work in the yard, I helped as much as I could. Whenever he would get in the car to go somewhere, I would run to jump in the car with him.

There was a longing for my dad's approval and acceptance. It didn't matter that up until I was twelve years old, my dad was a functioning alcoholic. He was my dad. He went to work every day, attended all our activities, and made sure there was food on the table. But there was still a void. When he came home, you never knew what mood he would be in, so we learned to adapt our behaviors and walk on eggshells, hoping none cracked. There was a price to pay for disobedience. Felicia knew how to stroke my dad's ego much better than we did. I think George always got the short end of the stick, which resulted in his resentment toward my dad. I wasn't far behind because my mouth kept me in trouble. Living with an alcoholic meant never knowing how his mood was going to be. My dad did not take any nonsense from us or anyone else. He demanded respect regardless of who you were. Everyone in the neighborhood knew not to bother Bill Turner or his household.

    My parents divorced when I was fourteen, and the grips of parental control were released. Unfortunately, I went from being in a controlled environment, to a less controlling environment, to being able to do as I pleased. After fourteen years of not being able to voice my opinion, I reached out to people to satisfy my own insecurities. By this time, I'd had many years of enabling an alcoholic father and emotionally enabling my mother and brother.

    Around the age of thirteen, George started to follow the wrong crowd, and became a victim of negative peer pressure, which resulted in him starting to use drugs. Due to his immature decisions, he began to sell drugs and got in trouble with the law. George always had a desire to be drug free even after countless failed attempts. A few months prior to George's passing, he went to Tennessee for a month to stay with my mom to clear his head and clean out his system. When he returned to Maryland, he came to stay with me for a few days. During his visit, he got a bad nose bleed so my mom took him to the emergency room. The physicians wanted to examine his inner stomach to ensure no blood was there, causing the matter to worsen. The nurse prepped him and inserted a tube in his mouth to pump his stomach. In doing so she inadvertently entered his lungs. They immediately admitted him into the hospital for a few days for observation and further testing. After being released from the hospital he went to visit his old neighborhood where he first started using drugs.

    No matter what, George always called my mom to let her know he was okay so she wouldn't worry. If George went more than eight hours and my mom didn't hear from him, she knew something was wrong, and April 7, 2013, was no different. A few hours after George went to visit his old neighborhood, my mother had an uneasy feeling so she called him and told him to be careful and that she loved him, and she asked him to come home. He said, "Okay," but, unfortunately, he never made it home.

    After a short while, my mom called a friend of George to see if he had seen or talked to him. He said no. She informed him that she was concerned because she hadn't heard from George in a while. George's friend asked my mom where was the last place she knew George was and she said on Iverson Street in Temple Hills, Maryland. He went around the neighborhood in search of George for my mother. When he finally got information on George's whereabouts, he was informed George had overdosed.

    I left work, and from inside my car, I started calling the local police stations and hospitals, inquiring about any deaths that might have been reported in the last few days fitting George's description. Felicia and I met at the Oxon Hill, Maryland, precinct to see if a body matching George's description had been found. When we arrived at the precinct, we were greeted by an officer and provided him a description of George as 6'2", 225 pounds, brown skin, beard, and numerous tattoos, but nothing was panning out. This gave me encouragement. After about fifteen minutes, the officer informed us that there is a body at the Chief Medical Examiner's Office in Baltimore that fits the description of George, but we would have to go to the Landover, Maryland, precinct first.

After leaving Oxon Hill with our minds in a whirlwind, Felicia and I arrived at the Landover precinct in Prince George's County, Maryland. I was still hoping the officer was mistaken, and that when we arrived, it wouldn't be George. Once there, my sister and I were taken to a back room with three detectives who began to question us about George's last whereabouts. After about twenty minutes of being questioned, I became agitated and asked why all the questions.

The detectives informed us that the coroner used his fingerprints from prior convictions to identify him, and confirmed it was George. We were informed he had overdosed two days prior. After answering questions that we thought were unnecessary for almost twenty minutes, feeling agitated and pissed, we had questions of our own that we wanted answered. We immediately questioned why didn't we get notified, and they informed us he didn't have any identification on him. We later learned after George's overdose his body was removed from the house he was in and left outside. His creden tials were taken as well because the person said they would contact the family but didn't.

For twenty-seven years, I enabled George's drug addiction, hoping what I was doing would help him, but I hindered his addiction. Enablement doesn't happen overnight. It started with the enabling of my parents, friends, and associates. By the time my dad and George had both passed, I had gone through a lot of trials and tribulations, which emotionally and physically drained me. I had hoped my actions, or should I say enabling, would've change the negative behaviors of others. I will share my lessons learned that hopefully might change the trajectory of your life, and help you avoid some of the major pitfalls I've encountered.

My mind replays the reality of my involvement in enabling George for years, and ultimately in his death; involvement that I want to forget. For some reason, I can't. I've processed it over and over: what I needed to say and do, but didn't. I allowed myself to enable him so long; I was emotionally invested in his dysfunctional behavior. The concerns I went to bed with woke me at three a.m. because I refused to address them the day prior. I've suppressed it in hopes that they vanish, as my dreams do, before I awake. It took me getting indignant with the consequences of my decisions that I started to make myself a priority, regardless of how it impacted others. I became my own advocate for happiness by changing my mindset and actions. You can too. You deserve to be free from bondage and the obligations to make everyone else happy.

To make changes, sometimes you must be willing to take the road least traveled. You must be your own advocate, and not conform to mediocrity. This road is typically for those who are self-motivated; the trailblazers and risk takers. Even so, this all comes with a cost of sometimes being ostracized by those you love. When I began to demonstrate tough love toward George and no longer enabled him, he initially viewed this as me being selfish "said that I was changing" but he knew I loved him.

This new journey can lead you into a period of isolation for a season, but never so long that you forget your desire to be connected and accepted. I compare this season to being out on a boat, sailing alone. Every so often, another ship will pass by and passengers wave to remind you that you're not alone. You see them from a distance, but your destination isn't the same. You may even begin to wonder why your journey doesn't allow for fleets of passengers to accompany you.

I thought sometimes that having a companion could make the

journey more enjoyable or the assignment go more quickly. I often asked myself, "What is there to learn from two ships passing in the night that keeps us holding on through life's journey?"

Some seasons last longer than others. You can experience both the joys of birth and the sorrows of death; so, embrace the seasons for what they are. You should live in the moment and not waste time. Through this life journey, it may appear that your navigation is off course because it's unfamiliar territory. As you remain consistent and keep the faith, you will inherently be steered in the right direction. The spiritual wind is guiding your sail to the appropriate destination. You don't have all the answers to every question, and you will make mistakes, but trust the process.

There have been times in my life I kept picking up hitchhikers (bad habits), so I wouldn't be alone. As the trip progressed, it became evident that wasn't my journey. So, once again, when I came to the end of myself, I stopped trying to force all the answers, and listened to my internal navigation system, and raised my anchor to sail on. Your spiritual compass will always reroute you when you deviate from the intended course. Your guide will orchestrate the route when you ask yourself, *where am I running?* And better yet, *What am I running from?* You stop long enough to acknowledge you've just

THE QUANDARY

had an epiphany. Your life's journey has come to the point where you realize you've been running from yourself.

What's going on in your life that makes you happy? Is it a person who covers up your guilty desires, a place toward which you gravitate, or a thing that brings you comfort? Wherever you go, you take yourself with you. Have joy and be content with yourself. Be content in the silence of your presence. Listen to the stillness of your future trying to be birthed and give you guidance on your next strategic move. You're so busy moving and shaking, you aren't sitting still long enough to allow your inner person the opportunity to speak. It's in the stillness of your day where you find peace and contentment. Identify your still place where you have no distractions. Your mind and heartbeat are all in one, setting in motion the endless parameters of your day. In this place, you must press through the initial feeling of being lonely and distracted. You're so used to everyone coming to you for advice and needing your opinion, it could feel awkward at first. You may think, *What do I do now? I'm not used to being by myself and just focusing on making me a priority.* Now it's time to be mentally and emotionally able to make wise, unwavering decisions.

There's a war being waged against you, and its sole purpose

is to destroy you by any means necessary. There are no rules in this fight, and anyone can distract you from your assignment. It's not good enough that you're saved, that you love people, or volunteer in your community. The enemy is coming for your peace, joy, finances, kids, and anything else positive that's a part of your life. The enemy wants to distract you in hopes of ultimately killing you in this fight.

One of the greatest joys for a parent is to raise a child to fulfill his or her life purpose. When we were infants, our parents had to do everything for us. They were so glad just to hear their child coo and smile. If we cried, it was up to them to decipher if we were wet or hungry. Parents had to meet our needs because we were unable to independently support ourselves. As we got older and matured, it was up to our parents to allow us to become more self-reliant. For example, if our parents continued to pacify our every need, they were producing a brat or a dependent child. For so many years this is what enabling parents have done.

As a parent, regardless of your social, economic, or financial status, you want the best for your child. I don't know any parent who doesn't have hopes and dreams for their child to be healthy and successful. There's a feeling of accomplishment in investing your time to shape the life of another and ultimately see the fruits of your labor.

THE QUANDARY

It's not about seeing your name on the marquee or getting the accolades, but rather knowing inwardly that you gave unconditionally to help make someone else better. True deposits never look for withdrawals.

I love roses. I believe they have the most beautiful appearance with a lovely aroma. The rose just doesn't become beautiful, season after season, without going through a pruning process. We, too, go through our own pruning process. God begins to cut back certain desires or people on whom we've become reliant. He removes them as our crutch, so we can become all He wants us to be. This process of pruning is uncomfortable, painful, and scary, and it can provide some uncertainty about where our stability is heading. The severing isn't designed to minimize your worth or growth potential. It's created to expand your capability to blossom and propel your potential. When gardeners prune roses, they do it just before the plant breaks dormancy after spring frost. They will cut back the bush in winter right before spring to enable its ability to grow higher and wider, beyond its original confinements. Your pruning process is designed to expand you and make you useful for this next season of your life. When you deviate from the process, you delay and potentially forfeit your assignment of being expanded to your full potential.

CHAPTER Two

Support vs. Enabling

No matter how many times I said yes to their requests, it was never enough. I didn't want anything in return from the people I helped, until their requests wouldn't cease. After years of doing for everyone else, I began to wonder who was truly there for me versus what I could do for them. The lines began to blur between my genuine desire to help and their overwhelming need to be provided for. Some people think that unconditional love means doing everything a person asks or tells them to do. That couldn't be further from the truth. The word of God in 1 Corinthians 13:4–8 says:

> *Love is patient, love is kind. It does not envy, it does not boast, it is not proud. [5] It does not dishonor others, it is not self-seeking, it is not easily an*

THE QUANDARY

> gered, it keeps no record of wrongs. ⁶ Love does not delight in evil but rejoices with the truth. ⁷ It always protects, always trusts, always hopes, always perseveres. ⁸ Love never fails. But where there are prophecies, they will cease; where there are tongues, they will be stilled; where there is knowledge, it will pass away.

I had to accept the true meaning of love, and then I needed to alter how I demonstrated it. We do many things in the name of love, but is it unconditional love or just seeking acceptance?

Love and support don't require you to say yes to being someone's doormat. The profound love we have toward those with whom we have relationships is immeasurable. Having standards is pivotal in any relationship. You should define your standards prior to encountering a situation or request. If you don't, you will find yourself giving out of your reserves to the point of being emotionally, physically, and/or financially bankrupt. You could also end up saying yes to everything; therefore, later find yourself feeling frustrated and overwhelmed with obligations. Our love for others can occasionally cripple us from maintaining a balanced lifestyle because we were too willing to say yes.

How do we go from loving and supporting others to enabling their destructive behaviors? In doing so, we begin to make decisions to carry their load in hopes it will change them for the best. In turn, it only perpetuates a cycle of dysfunction. How many of you woke up this morning, looked in the mirror, and said to yourself, *this would be a great day to start being an enabler*? Of course, you didn't.

Essentially, what I've been describing throughout this book is what licensed clinical psychotherapist Karen Allen terms as a personality disorder called "codependency." Defined by the *Diagnostic and Statistical Manual of Mental Health Disorders* (*DSM-5*), codependency, or being codependent, is "a pervasive and excessive need to be taken care of that leads to submissive and clinging behavior and fears of separation, beginning by early adulthood and present in a variety of contexts, as indicated by at least five (5) of the eight (8) criteria in the DSM-5" (see *DSM-5*, "Dependent Personality Disorder 301.6 Diagnostic Criteria").

This describes my brother perfectly. My immediate family members and I were the other half of the codependent relationship.

THE QUANDARY

We each:

- Had an excessive need to take care of him for fear of not having a relationship
- Provided an excessive amount of advice and reassurance
- Assumed responsibility for most major areas
- Feared losing the relationship if we didn't continue providing support (emotional and financial)
- Sought other unhealthy relationships
- Were preoccupied with fears of being left to take care of him if it came down to that

Let's look at the warning signs of an enabler:

Five Warning Signs of Being an Enabler:

- Saying yes just to appease others
- Always bailing them out of trouble
- Not being patient to allow them to confront the issue on their own
- Getting mad when they don't take your advice
- Doing for them what they should be doing for themselves

If you can answer yes to any of these warning signs, you could possibly be an enabler. Don't become distraught. There's help for you in this book. I am going to assist you with recognizing when you are making enabling decisions. Then you will create an action plan to address the root cause of why you make those decisions. Enabling is a learned behavior but you can unlearn it. If you put in the work, you can learn new, healthier behaviors that allow others to stand on their own two feet.

Being codependent is a full-time, exhausting job and has no long-term benefits. I say "long-term" because you do receive some temporary gratification for being an enabler or you wouldn't do it. We will discuss this later in the book.

Let's now take some time to identify the difference between supporting someone and enabling them. You can support a person financially, emotionally, physically, spiritually, or psychologically. As humans, we are relational beings and desire acceptance. When you support someone else's dreams, ambitions, and desires, it helps to form a bond between you and the other person. To truly support others is to help them do what they are not able to do for themselves. Let me say that again. Support is to help others do what they are not able to do for themselves. Keep in mind, I didn't say what they aren't "willing" to do for themselves. For example, you need a couch moved but it's too heavy, so you call your husband downstairs to move it. He has supported you with something you're not able to do for yourself. Maybe someone you know totaled her car and found

THE QUANDARY

herself without a vehicle to get around, so you allowed her to borrow your extra car for a few weeks until she purchased a new one. Showing support can be manifested in many forms, and it doesn't leave you with feeling drained, unappreciated, or depleted. Genuinely supporting others makes you feel empowered and liberated, because you've helped someone beyond their capacity.

Sometimes while desiring to be supportive, you can begin to teeter and cross the line into enabling. You may have the purest intentions, but the results of enabling are the same. Enabling is supporting habits and addictions that are detrimental to another person and yourself as well. When you enable others, you help them continue in self-destructive behaviors by providing excuses or by making it possible for them to avoid the consequences of their own behavior. Most people who enable put their own self-interests aside to appease others; then later regret it and complain. Typically, enablers can be easily manipulated.

If I had a dollar for every time I did something for someone when I didn't want to, I would be a millionaire. I have been an enabler for as long as I can remember. I recall in elementary school staying behind from recess to help clean out the desk of one of my close friends because it was so messy and he wouldn't do it himself.

SUPPORT VS. ENABLING

I would loan money (never to have it repaid) because I heard about a business deal that I just couldn't pass up. Maybe you can relate to what I've been through. I saw my brother use many types of drugs, which meant my years of being an enabler stretched beyond what I care to wish on my worst enemy.

Most enablers are in denial because they can't change what they don't acknowledge. If you are an enabler, this book is not designed to belittle you in any way. Its purpose is not to make you feel guilty, but it is designed to serve as an awakening to where you are; to help you acknowledge the behavior and make deliberate steps to change. Just know that change is possible, but it doesn't happen overnight. It doesn't matter if you have been an enabler for thirty days or forty-five years. If you have breath in your body, you can make the change in your decisions and live again, for you.

I pray as you read this book that you allow yourself to be open and honest about your life's choices, the situations you are in, and the decisions you are making. I'm going to be transparent about the many enabling decisions I'd made in hopes of you not having to repeat my mistakes. Often you aren't an enabler to just one person, but it's a lifestyle that needs to be altered.

The foundation of any relationship should be built on

THE QUANDARY

common respect, trust, acceptance, and appreciation. My dad used to tell us, "If you make your bed hard, you must lie in it." He meant it. There was no enabling on his part. I thought that was the meanest statement a parent could make to his or her child. I thought the responsibility of parents was to love, support, pay the bills, and make life easier for their child. By the way, we didn't ask to be born. How many times have you said that under your breath, while getting in trouble? It wasn't until I became an adult and reflected on that statement that I became accountable for the decisions I make. Sometimes I get it right and sometimes I don't. I tell my daughters all the time that regardless of their decisions, right or wrong, they are accountable for their consequences. Scripture says, "You shall reap that which you sow."

Although I learned this firm belief from my dad, my mother was the opposite. My mom was the enabler who always wanted to help everyone regardless of who they were, or if it was for the best. She never met a stranger who didn't need her assistance. She would give her last to make sure everyone was happy, and taken care of. My mother was an enabler, because she was taught by her mother who was an enabler, and so the cycle continued. My grandmother was married to an alcoholic, and my mother, in turn, married an alcoholic. Thank God when I was around the age of thirteen, my dad went to Alcoholics Anonymous, and never drank again. As I said before, you can't change what you don't acknowledge. I'm hoping by writing this book and dealing with my insecurities that my daughters will not repeat the cycle. Now that we know better, we should do better. I believe in the name of Jesus that the curse of codependency stops with me.

As a teenager, I recall praying to God, "You can take my life if you would only deliver George from drugs." I was so emotionally broken to see the downward spiral my brother had taken. At a young age, I thought it was my responsibility to save him from himself. I had put more stake into his life than I had into my own. I was willing to die for him, and he was already killing himself. I started to become his little "god."

One of the characteristics of an enabler is being indecisive. I was forever going back on my word. The word of God calls that "unstable." God's word says in James 1:8, "A double minded man is unstable in all his ways." Being indecisive was second nature to me. I told my brother a million times, "Don't come asking me for any more money." I knew deep down inside he wouldn't do anything, but smoke or shoot up, but I was in denial, as if he would finally do the right thing. But he would come up with a compelling story that weighed on my heart and I gave in again. I loved him so much and wasn't willing or able to practice tough love yet. I would fuss the whole time while giving him money or taking him where he wanted to go. I broke more promises to myself that I stopped believing in the decisions I was making. I remember a good friend once told me to stop saying what I was or wasn't going to do; allow your actions to show it.

    Finally, a light bulb went off, and I had to look internally and understand: why couldn't I follow through? I thought to myself, *don't keep being weak and woman up.* I had to realize there were some inadequacies within me that made me focus so much on enabling others that I didn't want to self-reflect.

    Being an enabler is like running a three-legged race heading in opposite directions. If you've ever run a three-legged race, you know the importance of selecting the right partner. Your weakness should be your partner's strength, and you need to stay focused and work together toward a common goal. These strategies are important to avoid continuously falling and ultimately losing the race. When selecting who's on your team, it's helpful if you are both approximately the same height. You should have the same destination in mind. It is impossible to be tied together and have different destinations in mind. Can you imagine being tied to the ankle of the person you are enabling when he or she starts running left, but you start running right? It won't work because being connected to another person and supporting him or her requires an agreement on destination. If you are not in agreement with the direction, you will go tumbling—financially, emotionally, mentally, physically, and psychologically. What will it take for you to snip the bandage that's holding your ankles together and allow the other person to run his or her own race?

Take your time to reflect on the Action Plan questions and answer them truthfully. Your change is only as authentic as your answers.

THE QUANDARY

Your Action Plan

Identify at least one area in your life where you are being an enabler:

_____

_____

_____

_____

_____

_____

_____

What story are you telling yourself to justify why you are continuing in this behavior?

_____

_____

_____

_____

_____

_____

_____

SUPPORT VS. ENABLING

Your Action Plan

List three changes you will make immediately to hold the other person accountable for his or her own actions:

_____
_____
_____
_____
_____
_____
_____
_____

Name an accountability partner to support you:

_____
_____
_____
_____
_____
_____
_____

THE QUANDARY

CHAPTER *Three*

Wanting More for You

Your self-progress starts with a single day. You can never accomplish your dreams or complete an assignment without a beginning. So many people want to arrive or obtain the prize without any effort. Putting in the work is necessary to having the life you want. How do you handle it when you want more for others than they want for themselves? It's challenging when you see so much potential in others, yet they never seem to muster the strength to make the decisions for positive results. There's this merry-go-round effect in their lives where no progression is being made. They aren't passing their tests, yet you decide to bail them out again. What you think is helping them is actually hindering their progression toward maturity and liberation.

They go to work on time for the first few months and easily

lose stamina to maintain a schedule and commitment. They start showing up to work late and get written up for excessive tardiness and absenteeism. For one reason or another, they always have an excuse for why it's not their fault. There's an inability on their part to take ownership of their decisions. There is always a plan B in their book, which is you. They are waiting for you to bail them out. But why should they have to be accountable when you're their enabler, their get-out-of-jail free card, just like in Monopoly. What started off as assertiveness quickly became laziness and lack of effort. They're too tired from hanging out all night to get to work on time. The decisions they've made have now led them to being terminated.

So, the cycle continues. People who make decisions with only today in mind become stagnant, unable to see beyond their immediate need. People who live for the moment tend to associate with others who aren't visionaries. There are no thoughts or progressive actions toward future goals of buying their own home or car, saving for retirement, or putting money aside for a rainy day. Even if you live paycheck to paycheck, you should have a plan. I know what it's like to not have money for groceries. I've had to borrow from family and friends to buy groceries for my children before. Then in turn, if I borrowed, I always paid it back. I then had to look at my house hold finances and make different decisions about how I spent my money. It's not about how much you earn, it's about what you're doing with your money. You can earn over $100,000, but if you haven't learned how to manage your spending, you can still end up broke.

It's a mindset and a discipline knowing that the decisions you make today will determine your destination tomorrow. Nothing goes unchallenged, because the universe is designed to create what you speak and do. The word of God says you have what you say. It's not countered by "I was just kidding."

I know there are some "super" Christians who are probably thinking the word of God also says in Matthew 6:34, "So don't worry about tomorrow, for tomorrow will bring its own worries. Today's trouble is enough for today." If taken out of context, you would give yourself an excuse not to work the plan. Life owes no one anything. The word also says in Habakkuk 2:2, "Write the vision, and make it plain upon tablets, that he may run that readeth it." There are some people you are trying to help who think they do not have to make the necessary sacrifices to be self-sufficient. They want to rely on you to do everything when the plan doesn't work.

I knew a lady—let's call her Sharon—who was dating a very

THE QUANDARY

popular guy named Tim. He was a great dresser, the life of the party, and handsome, but he had a gambling issue. Three to four days a week, you could find him at the casino or some firehouse gambling. Some days he would win big, and things at home were great. When Tim lost, which sometimes included their rent money, things at home were not so great. Sharon was fine with the gambling when Tim came home with expensive gifts, but when he lost big, she was ready to leave him. Gambling impacted her livelihood by losing their rent money and other essential payments for bills. For a person to stay in a dysfunctional relationship there is a win in it for them. Sometimes it requires you to be alone and dig deep to ask yourself, *Why I am continuing in this toxic relationship?* No one does anything detrimental to his or her own peace without getting something out of the deal.

As chaotic as your situation may be, you wouldn't be there if you didn't get something from the relationship. Maybe your win is acceptance, and by staying, you have someone who idolizes you. The other person needs you to tell him or her what to do. This gives you the temporary acceptance you need to feel empowered, but it's coming at a high cost. In the example of Sharon and Tim, her win was that she enjoyed the nicer things in life and the prestige that came with the lifestyle. It exposed her to a social crowd she couldn't afford without Tim. She had to pay the cost of instability, which resulted in her getting high blood pressure, bad credit, and embarrassment, especially when the eviction notice was left on the front door. What cost are you willing to pay to be an enabler?

For me, being an enabler was a generational curse. I saw how my grandfather would control others, and it was his way or the highway. To maintain a relationship with him, you had to comply with his rules. I know the balancing act it takes to walk in an unstable emotional environment, not quite knowing the mood of the person on the other side of the door. You mentally prepare yourself and remain adaptable until you observe the surroundings and adjust accordingly. I spent many years of my life enabling others just for peace. I thought it was my responsibility to take care of everyone. I would date guys just because they were Christians and went to church, they were handsome, and I saw their potential, but later I learned there was more to hope for. I avoided all the warning signs that this wasn't the person for me. Enabling is a tiring and endless job. You never get off duty. At least when you go to work, you know your work hours. At some point, you get off work and walk out the door, but as an enabler you are on duty 24/7, 365 days a year.

THE QUANDARY

In my own eyes, I saw myself as George's second mom. With that status, I made decisions detrimental to my life and I felt responsible for what wasn't mine. I took responsibility for his actions and was vulnerable. George had a way of frustrating me and making me laugh all at the same time. He loved his family, but loved the streets equally. He would transform his life as a chameleon does in the wild. I always say everyone has two sides. Your connection to me will determine whether your access is to my personal or professional world. I loved the half of George's world that I knew and understood. But I could never understand the other half of his life he had to live based on his decisions. There was a price I know he didn't want to pay. The part we knew and loved was that of a generous and compassionate person, but there was another side to George.

George was a tall, handsome, popular, outgoing man, who made friends easily. He was athletic and would do anything for anyone. When George was growing up, I always recall him dating females who had kids. I would laugh when I asked him, "Do you know anyone who doesn't have a child?" Here comes George into the house with his new female friend and her baby. I never tried to memorize anyone's name because there were so many females in his life. Because I loved kids, George knew I would be his babysitter while he entertained his company. I prayed over every child I held that when they grew up, they would love God and be healthy.

George was a die-hard Washington Redskins fan and a father. My mother and I raised Kaylah like our own. He grew up tumbling at Green Valley elementary school and playing basketball throughout his life. George existed by living a double life. Like the chameleon transforms to adapt to life, so did George. Every time he was incarcerated we financially supported his lifestyle with the latest fashions and kept his commissary full. We found out later that he was selling some of the commissary items for profit. Entrepreneurship is popular in the prison system. I bought numerous televisions for him to have while incarcerated, only to have him leave the gifts for the next inmate to keep.

Every time he got arrested, I took the responsibility to contact the bail bondsman to get him out. Only to be let down when he repeatedly committed the same offense. I'd given him money to pay off debts to drug dealers so they would not physically harm him. He suffered from being alienated and isolated from friends, sometimes not knowing where he would sleep next. This was very heartbreaking because this was the life he chose.

Sometimes you may never understand the decisions a person

makes. George didn't like to mix his two worlds. Nothing stopped me when it came to the health and security of my brother. I recall going to the drug house at night looking for him. I drove up nervously, thinking, *what in the hell are you doing out here?* I slowly got out of the car, walked down the sidewalk, and asked someone outside, "Is George, or 'G,' inside the building?" Most of the time, the person I asked would say no, but I've learned there's a street code at all levels.

I have visited George in more jails in Maryland than I care to remember. I've been everywhere from Upper Marlboro to Jessup to Baltimore to Hagerstown to Sykesville, and possibly one or two others; even visited some twice. This was all before I was twenty-five years old. Sometimes there was comfort for us knowing George was incarcerated and alive, rather than on the streets dead. I know this seems like an oxymoron, but until you've walked in the shoes of addictive family member, you may never understand. I was mentally drained before even having my first child. I felt I had already gone through the terrible teenage years of a child. In high school, I recall telling my mom, "I divorce you." I could no longer be her emotional support system. I made sacrifices for the sake of love, but to the extent of enablement.

As I reflect on growing up, I would always say George was the nicest of the three of us. He was a born giver. He loved our mom, Felicia, and me. Never would he come into our presence without giving a hug and kiss. He was a momma's boy to the core. My mom found joy in George. I always teased her, and said he was her favorite child. He provided her the love she didn't receive from others. George loved himself some Sandra Turner (Mom). My mom was so in tuned with George, she knew when something was wrong with him. She was so connected to him, she could sense his pain and hurt, which caused her to hurt. My mother could discern hardship coming to George and would try to warn him. Sometimes he listened; sometimes he did not. His worst afflictions were brought on himself. As a family, we endured a lot, but love kept us together.

I wanted to help push George toward a purpose, so I gave and gave until I was depleted emotionally and became angry. What I began to realize is that I don't have the capability to birth anything in anyone other than myself. God gives some to plant and some to water, but He gets the increase. I had to begin to put things in their proper perspective. It's not our job to guilt-trip, manipulate, or control anyone into doing anything outside of his or her own will. Our job is to pray and trust God.

THE QUANDARY

If you are honest with yourself, is the person you continue to bail out able to conceptualize tomorrow's decisions without you rescuing them or you telling them what to do? When a woman gives birth through a C-section the doctor instructs her the next day to start walking to rebuild her core muscles. Because she doesn't want to endure the pain she decides to lay around. What could have healed in 4-6 weeks now takes 8-10 weeks. It's up to you on how long it takes to heal. Only the temporary discomfort of standing, bending, and walking strengthens the core to heal. If you decide to stay in your comfort zone, on the couch, despite the doctor's orders to regain strength will only hinder your ability to bounce back quickly. Now, here comes your enabler, as your plan B. While on the couch, despite doctor orders, you have everything brought to you. You go to the extreme to text them every five minutes when you need something. They stay on the couch so long they lose all strength to stand on their own; which prolongs their recovery.

Take your hands off the process. You are circumventing God's ordained development and substituting your own. You can't change anyone, but yourself. I know this sounds like a cliché, but it's true. We are programmed to think that if we just do a little more, pray another prayer, fast once again, it could be the one thing that could change the person you're enabling. I don't know about you, but I got tired of fasting for others who didn't really want to change. I was sitting there praying and fasting, and they were at the buffet line eating like there was no tomorrow. Take that weight off yourself. You were not equipped to handle the weight of your family. Give them to God.

One lesson that liberated me was the concept of coming into agreement with another person. It is an essential component when wanting to connect or partner with someone toward receiving a desired outcome. It could entail agreeing with a prayer request, finances, an emotional situation, or something else. Matthew 18:19 states, "I also tell you this: If two of you agree on earth concerning anything you ask, my Father in heaven will do it for you." I have learned when someone asks me to pray, I ask them what their prayer request is for. I need to make sure I can agree with what they are hoping to receive. Coming into agreement is sometimes touching, agreeing in thought, word, and action in a common request. There are some exceptions when a person isn't specific, because of confidentiality, but then, you can never go wrong just praying the word. Every prayer request you receive may not be in your best interest. As the two of you continue converse, he may tell you he fell in love with a

THE QUANDARY

married woman and he can't live without her. He's been dating her for eight months and knows he shouldn't have crossed the line, but he's convinced that she is supposed to be his wife and God brought them together. Now he wants you to pray with him that she will leave her husband for him and they can live happily ever after. This may be an instance where you don't want to get involved. You can't afford to enter into agreements haphazardly. Your words create your realities. Per the above scripture, if any two-people come into agreement about anything, it could happen. That's the power of our words. So many people speak contrary to what they want, thinking sarcasm is funny and won't manifest what they've spoken. The universe is designed to bring forth that which you decree out of your mouth. It's not what you think, but what you speak. When you connect with another like-minded person, whether good or bad, the universe is designed to bring forth what you said.

Let's say you meet the woman of your dreams. She's five-foot-nine with beautiful long hair and is a partner at her law firm. She loves sports and has a figure like a Roman goddess. It was attraction at first sight. You ask her on a date and the two of you hit it off right away. One date leads to two, and the next thing you know, you've been dating for two years. You love her and don't want to go another year just courting her. You've saved your money, and it's now time to pop the big question and ask her to marry you. Her response to your proposal will determine if she comes into agreement to be your wife. How you live together and handle the marital affairs will require many more agreements. Who is the best person to manage the household finances? Will you have a joint account or separate accounts? Do you want children? What church will you attend? All these questions will require agreements.

I recall being a single parent and believing in the power of agreement. When I read the scripture on touching and agreeing, it didn't say there was an age requirement. I would take my five-year-old daughter by the hand, tell her what we needed for our lives, and pray. I saw God open supernatural doors for us. I went from borrowing money to having a savings account. I also saw the power of agreeing with someone who made detrimental decisions, and I suffered the consequences of those agreements.

Many would love to believe their decisions have no bearing on anyone other than themselves. This couldn't be further from the truth. Because we are social beings, we feel others' pleasures, pains, joys, and sorrows. All too often I've seen how a person wants you to mind your own business until they need you. It's like, *do what I asked*

THE QUANDARY

you to do, and then back off. Perhaps you've been in a situation when someone came to borrow money from you because he couldn't meet his monthly obligations. He is overextended month after month. There's more month than money. You volunteer to help him set a budget and all you hear is, "Mind your business" and "Don't tell me what to do." He refuses to apply for other career opportunities that would position him to be financially independent. In turn, he keeps borrowing money month after month to make ends meet, with no plan for getting out of debt. This is only perpetuating the cycle to being in worse debt the following month. Life's situations are real. Supporting people through their decisions is admirable, but enabling their dysfunctional behaviors is crippling.

There comes a time when you should have a come-to-Jesus moment to face reality. Allow them to reap the consequences of their actions. This has allowed me to release control from feeling obligated to be their crutches. This process wasn't easy because, as an enabler, I wanted to fix things and people. I mentally put them on the potter's wheel to shape them for my masterpiece. In the back of my mind, I already pictured what they should be doing, what they should have achieved, and where they should be going. I thought it wouldn't happen without my assistance. Again, demonstrating the god complex. Remembering, when I cried to God and said, "You can take my life if you will just save and deliver George. God, you can do anything, so why haven't you done this yet?" Although I was being genuine, I was ignorant of God's process. I meant it to the core of my being, but I thank God, he didn't take my life. Although I was a good, law-abiding person, I hadn't accepted Jesus as the Savior of my life at that time. Being a good person doesn't get you into heaven, but accepting Him as Lord and Savior will.

There are times when you enable a behavior because you want to fit in. I've had to learn the hard way about trying to fit in with the hopes of being accepted. I would go above and beyond to be nice, alter my personality, speak softer, volunteer more, and pay when the bill came. I wasn't being my authentic self but trying to be who others wanted me to be. I would try to speak softly, only to find that I was frustrated in the end because I'm naturally a loud talker, so I've come to live with it. Growing up, I was always outspoken and said what I thought. This got me into more trouble than I care to remember. I've always kept to small groups because I don't like confusion. Sometimes as Christians, we try to prove we are so spiritual by setting up our calendars to be at everything just so others won't judge us. We attend all Sunday services, every meeting, whether it's

THE QUANDARY

your ministry or not, Bible study, and don't let us forget to give everyone a hug. If we don't, they might think we are mad at them or jealous. That's the most ridiculous thing because nobody jealous of you. You're just trying too hard to fit in.

I recall trying to be the best leader, employee, girlfriend, and friend, only to find out I was failing miserably. I was trying too hard to make sure all my 'I's were dotted and 'T's crossed, instead of letting it flow. The more I tried to fit in, the less I felt accepted. So I started to question why I didn't fit in. I thought, I'm a good person and I love the Lord. I give, I support, and I'm committed, but something within was tugging at me to say, "Warning—something isn't right."

One Saturday morning, I was sitting in the living room just being quiet and my spirit told me to look up the definitions of "fitting in" and "belonging." I thought this was interesting because initially I thought they meant the same thing. One definition of "fitting in" means to conform. I thought, *Conform to what?* So I looked up "belonging," which means to be rightly placed in a specified position. I thought, *That's it. I've been asking for the wrong thing. I've been asking all this time to fit in, which explains why I've been conforming to what everyone wants me to be, needing approval and acceptance.*

When you know better, you do better. When your aim is to fit in, you have agreed to standards that are beneath you. Wanting to fit in allows you only to conform to mediocrity and not to fulfill your true potential. Are you afraid to say no, feeling as if you're letting people down and at risk of eliminating another relationship? Whether you're married or single, there are certain expectations we put on ourselves or allow others to put on us. Make sure those expectations are attainable, and not one-sided. My new mantra is "No more time for one-sided relationships."

Genuine friendships just flow. It doesn't mean you won't have disagreements, but they survive the test of time. There are no pretenses or ultimatums in being true friends. Friends just accept you for who you are and all your experiences. If you're the only one making the phone calls, picking up the bill, and being the encourager, you are in the wrong circle. When God leads you to pull back from a person, it's for a reason. Relationships are designed to be for a reason, season, or lifetime. Accept their purpose and don't try to force a closed season open. God would never ask you to do anything or give up something that will hurt you. It's always for your good. If you do not willingly walk away from a bad relationship, it will cost you dearly later. Our sense of belonging can never be greater than our

THE QUANDARY

level of self-acceptance. The liberty of our life is based upon the choices we make.

Life is not easy, but it's meant to be enjoyed. If the blessings of God are limitless, why do we place limitations on what we can obtain or accomplish? Is it because our finite minds are not able to conceptualize beyond what we can physically see? The word of God says that as far as your eyes can see, you can possess if you only believe. Sometimes it takes encouraging yourself and speaking contrary to what your flesh is feeling or currently seeing. For me, when I find myself internalizing negative information I begin to make my situation appear worse than what it is. I would have taken a small issue, and by the time I'm done thinking about it, I've created a dramatic scenario out of nothing. I don't know about you, but my mind can wander to the point where I've created a motion picture. I just count it as my creative side that needs discipline. I wish that I were so disciplined to immediately bring every thought into captivity and focus on the positive, but that isn't the case all the time. It takes me a minute.

There's always been something within me that has made me know there's destiny inside me. You have that same drive that hasn't allowed you to give up, despite your situation. We are called to greatness; sometimes greatness is cultivated in isolation. I never understood that until God began to remove people from my life that I prayed He would allow to stay. God has called us to live a victorious life without condemnation. Sometimes God removes people from our lives because He knows we would never remove them ourselves. When God closes that door to the relationship you wanted, do not wallow in self-defeat and pity. Learn the lesson and move on.

If anyone can overthink or overanalyze a situation, that would be me. It got to the point that I got on my own nerves. That's sad to say but true. Then one day I told myself, *it's time to make different decisions* and *grow up. Acknowledge your mistakes and forgive yourself.* I was good at forgiving others, but horrible at forgiving myself. I had a perfectionist complex, thinking I shouldn't make any mistakes. I would tell myself, *That was so dumb. I can't believe you did that.* This gave the enemy access to enter my head and place other negative thoughts. Everyone exhibits stress very differently. Mine showed up as overeating, yelling, feeling frustrated, or surrounding myself with people to enable. I had allowed similar spirits to connect to me instead of seeking inward healing and deliverance.

Regardless of how strong and delivered you think you are, if you are in toxic relationships or environments, either they will

THE QUANDARY

change you or you will change them. It depends who's the stronger of the two. I recall telling myself, *If I haven't found the right person to enjoy life with, then I would enjoy it alone, until the right person comes along. You must be comfortable being alone before you can be suitable to be a mate.* I love "me time." I can go anywhere by myself. I travel alone; go to dinner, the theatre, church; and work out at the gym alone. I would love to have a life partner one day, but if it doesn't happen, it will not paralyze me. My happiness is not contingent on anyone other than me. There are some blessings awaiting you to which no one else can contribute. So, ask yourself: will you go alone to achieve your own happiness, or are you willing to wait and possibly forfeit your chance?

    I believe in small steps until you're able to take leaps and bounds. I didn't start off flying to Puerto Rico alone for a week, and going kayaking at night with strangers. I started off going to a movie and dinner alone. Then I took a train ride to New York for a Broadway play to see *Kinky Boots* featuring my cousin. I desire to go to London and Africa in the next few years. If I don't have anyone to join me, I will be getting on the plane by myself. When you break free from being an enabler, your entire mindset shifts to new possibilities. I've made up my mind that God gave me this life, and it's okay if no one else shares my interests. God created me to be unique and set apart, and I couldn't allow others to stop my growth and enjoyment of life; neither should you.

What have you always wanted to do but are afraid to do? What excuses have you told yourself why you can't live your dreams? Maybe you have a book waiting to be written or a song within you that needs to be birthed. You should press forward beyond your comfort zone, and don't spend all your time enabling others to fulfill their dreams. Stop bailing your grown children out of trouble and allow them to be independent. I know it's hard and it requires you to be disciplined, have tenacity and fortitude not to concede, but trust me it works. It's easy to make excuses and blame others for why you can't stop enabling. You could think: if they would only stop asking it would be easier. You're so busy doing for everyone else, but not seeing how it's impacting you. Once you get over the fear and overthinking, it will become easier with each decision you need to make. There's purpose within you; watch the hand of God orchestrate your steps. Don't overthink it; just move. There are limitless blessings for you.

As I was sitting and typing by the lake, I threw a piece of bread out for the ducks to eat, and their actions astonished me. One duck made a deep quacking sound to signify for all the other ducks to come and partake. One by one, each duck took a piece of the bread that was floating in the water and then moved on. There was enough to go around. One duck wasn't trying to hoard all the bread or feed the other ducks, but they all took responsibility for what was available. The same is true for us. If we just collaborate with each other and share our gifts and talents, and hold others accountable, there's enough "bread" to go around. I've worked hard to end the cycle of enablement, and I continue to make daily decisions to do better.

Take your time to reflect on the Action Plan questions and answer them truthfully. Your change is only as authentic as your answers.

Your Action Plan

Name the behavior you are trying to change in someone.

_____
_____
_____
_____
_____
_____
_____

How is that behavior working for you?

_____
_____
_____
_____
_____
_____
_____

THE QUANDARY

Your Action Plan

What are the dreams you are avoiding by putting all your attention on someone else?

_____
_____
_____
_____
_____
_____
_____
_____

What do you need to start doing to accomplish your goals?

_____
_____
_____
_____
_____
_____
_____
_____

CHAPTER *Four*

Truth or Manipulation

Discernment is a powerful inner instrument we've been given to detect the truth from a lie. It's comparable to walking around with your own personal deception detection device. You don't need to strap someone down and drill them with questions. Discernment gives you the ability to judge well.

1 Thessalonians 5:22–23 says, "But examine everything carefully; hold fast to that which is good; abstain from every form of evil." The apostle John issues a similar warning when he says, "Do not believe every spirit, but test the spirits to see whether they are from God; because many false prophets have gone out into the world." Your discernment is more reliable than a polygraph test. The intent of a lie detector is to get to the truth by asking specific questions. The findings can be manipulated based on the person's expe-

THE QUANDARY

rience with being deceptive. There's something about having the gift of discernment; it bypasses all deceptive abilities and perceives the spirit of the person and if they're being truthful.

Utilizing your discernment provides you the ability to differentiate the truth from fabrication simply by being tapped into the Spirit of God and receptive to the answer you receive. Some who don't believe in God call this their intuition or gut feeling. As an enabler, you don't always want to know the truth. You want to hear what pacifies your concerns, but that contaminates the findings.

To truly be free, you must remove your masks to face reality and acknowledge your truths. So, if your truth is that to start your day you must drink alcohol, acknowledge it. This could be the only means by which you can start your day and function. You may have to accept that you could be an alcoholic and need intervention. This doesn't make you a bad person, but it just means something has a stranglehold on you. Maybe your actions could be negatively impacting your friends and loved ones. Perhaps your children are acting out in school because they're concerned about your welfare. Life would be wonderful if you could just confess your issue, say a quick prayer, and have everything magically become perfect. In most instances, it doesn't happen that quickly. It is during the process you begin to make life-altering decisions. You decide not to go to the liquor store to purchase alcohol, but instead buy juice, water, or tea. Instead of getting short tempered and striking your wife, you go for a walk to clear your head and deescalate your anger.

It's natural to want your needs met, but most manipulators use underhanded, deceptive tactics to get their way. Manipulation is used to change the perception or behavior of others by self-motivated deceptive, tactics. By advancing the interests of the manipulator, often at another's expense, such methods could be considered exploitative, abusive, and underhanded. Manipulators may appear sincere, or genuine, as if the person has your best interest. Typically, their behavior is meant to achieve their own motive. You may not realize that you're being subconsciously controlled.

There are some manipulators who know how to tell an enthralling story that leaves you believing they will die, be evicted, become homeless, or starve in the next twenty minutes if you don't give them what they've asked for. I know that seems extreme but it's true. Some people are master manipulators and everything is urgent. Just tell them, "The lack of planning on your end doesn't constitute an emergency on mine." Some manipulators conjure up a tactic to start an argument just to blame you for something you didn't do in order to get their way. They want to have power over you so that ultimately you will do what they want. When you become wise to their tactics, you can change the game plan.

The truth is, most times you know deep down inside when someone isn't telling the truth. Ladies, how many times have you asked your significant other if you look like you've lost weight? You know you haven't been exercising or cutting back on your caloric intake. You just want him to tell you what you want to hear. Because he loves you and wants peace in the house, he says, "Yes, sweetie." We do it all the time. Now let's say you've been married for twelve years. Your relationship is relatively healthy, but every time your husband does anything you don't like, you withhold sex from him like a dangling carrot. You begin to manipulate him with a form of intimacy. This is misusing the covenant of marriage as a manipulation tool to teach him a lesson: *do as I want or else.* Using this type of underhanded tactic can backfire. Use another consequence and enjoy your good thing.

When you feel responsible for what's not yours you feel guilty, so you find yourself doing what you don't want to do. Many times, in codependent relationships, you don't want to be the bad guy and address the issue or say no. You want peace, so you leave the conversation for another day. You want everyone to like and accept you, so you bail them out until it becomes overwhelming. That's when all hell breaks loose and you're ready to throw the baby out with the bath water. You've had enough. You are paying a hefty cost for your need for acceptance and approval.

My breaking point as an enabler was when I started seeing everything I cared about falling apart all around me. I could no longer juggle all the balls and keep them in the air. I was yelling at the kids and complaining about having to do everything as a single parent. I was stretched too thin from all of my responsibilities. I just cried. I was out of balance and needed to recalibrate my priorities.

In life, you can't put all your faith and trust in a person, because we are human and make mistakes. If your happiness is based on what someone else says or does, then you are putting your reliance on an imperfect person to meet your needs. This can cause you to be set up for true disappointment. What are those prayer requests you wrote down and asked God for? You say you want one thing, but keep accepting the opposite when he comes walking past. Are you asking God to send you Boaz but you keep dating guys contrary because it gives you immediate gratification and something to do? This guy always has an excuse why he can't take you out and he is not emotionally available to you. You don't need discernment for this. You just need to run and take heed to the warning signs that you're about to enter an enabling relationship. I'm all for partnership, but be truthful about what you want and wait for it. Recognize the character of a man or woman before you allow that person into your heart.

Among the core characteristics of codependency, the most common theme is an excessive reliance on other people for approval and identity. One key sign of excessive reliance is when your sense of purpose in life is wrapped around making extreme sacrifices to satisfy another's needs. I come from a family with codependency behaviors. We all have been enablers in our relationships with each other, but daily we are making the strides to live healthier lives.

When George first got high, he was introduced to it from a family member. I'm sure he had no idea it would become an evolving habit, and eventually lead to his death. It was because of George's addiction that led to many of his incarcerations. From the age of 14 to the age of 40 the longest George ever was out of jail was two consecutive years. It was like the prison had revolving doors, When George needed money, no matter his condition, we would give it. Sometimes just to make sure he ate or had money for personal items. My mother would allow George to borrow her car, only for him to turn around and total it, and she was left with nothing to drive. I allowed her to drive my second car until I could buy her another vehicle. When George was younger, my mother allowed him to continue living in her home even though she knew he sold drugs because she didn't want to put him out. He would offer her money but she would not take it. His addiction became so bad he began selling her property to the pawn shop, and she had to pay to get it back. In George's mind, he didn't see anything wrong with what he did. He felt the items were on loan, and my mom could get her stuff when he got more money.

Karen Allen believes "an enabler happens for many reasons, as previously described; more often than not, it occurs out of a warped sense of love and concern for the person being enabled. You CAN love someone to a fault."

What will it take for us to accept the truth? The truth will set you free. At least that's what I've been told. The truth isn't always easy to accept or deal with. Being an enabler for twenty-seven years to someone with an addiction wasn't an easy life. One time drug dealers were in my mother's house because George owed them money. My mother came home and knew by their demeanor they were drug dealers. They were trying to be polite but her discernment kicked in. My mother casually went in the kitchen, called her nephew on the phone, and got a knife. She stood within view of George's company without them seeing her. She started talking loudly, hitting the table with the knife at the same time, so they could hear her loud and clear. She yelled, "There are these drug dealers in my house, and if they don't get out, they will die!" Next thing you know, the living room cleared out. I thank God for keeping my mom and myself safe during our foolish attempts at trying to save George. I wouldn't encourage anyone to do the things we did, but love makes you do things you later regret.

Be wise and know everyone who calls you "mom" or "friend" doesn't always have your best interest at heart. It is sometimes those so-called friends who provide you with bad advice or expect you to enable their destructive behavior. Separate yourself from anything or anyone who isn't a true friend. I believe George knew his last days were near because he began to apologize and make amends with people he had hurt and mistreated throughout the years. I share my intimate experiences hoping you live one day fewer an enabler than I did.

Take your time to reflect on the Action Plan questions and answer them truthfully. Your change is only as authentic as your answers.

Your Action Plan

What truths aren't you willing to face?

_____

_____

_____

_____

_____

_____

_____

_____

How will you handle it differently when you know someone is being manipulative?

_____

_____

_____

_____

_____

_____

_____

_____

THE QUANDARY

CHAPTER *Five*

Trust the Process

Trusting the process can feel as if you're riding the biggest and tallest roller coaster at the slowest speed possible. You're buckled in the seat of your situation, and all you can do is hold on tight and trust that the manufacturer designed the ride well. To your surprise, this roller coaster takes you up, down, around sharp turns, up steep hills, forward, reverse, and upside down. Observing others on the journey never gives you an accurate depiction of what the ride truly entails. When you're an onlooker, it appears fun, thrilling, and adventurous, and all too quickly it's your turn to go through. Just when you thought you had everything lined up in your life, you become closer to being next. The kids are starting to act right, your husband is showing you more affection, and you just got a raise at your job. That's just the time the roller coaster operator signals for you to

THE QUANDARY

board the ride. You're excited, your adrenaline is pumping, and you're anticipating the excitement you're about to experience. What you thought would be a thrill of a lifetime and over within sixty seconds turns out to be the lesson of a lifetime.

Nothing about going through a process is fast. On day one, it is easy to cope, but on day 365, your change still hasn't happened. What do you do now? Your emotions begin to go topsy-turvy. You realize you don't have any control over how fast you will receive what you need. Just buckle in and hold on. Believe that every turn, dip, and fall you're about to encounter will produce purpose, character, and a testimony. By the time, you get off this ride, you will be whole, lacking nothing. The ride may not end in ninety seconds like you thought, or maybe not even nine years, but keep pressing.

The definition of process is a systematic order in doing something that will result in an outcome. When you totally surrender to the process, you relinquish your control to God's will. Regardless of the outcome, you know it worked out the way it was supposed to, and you have no regrets.

Let me share a story with you about how it was good that I was afflicted. The scriptures tell us in Psalms 119:71, "It was good for me to be afflicted so that I might learn your status." I had to allow the process to work for me. Sometimes your troubles are not about you. In life, we will all encounter trials and tribulations. It's not what happens to us that matters, but how we respond that makes the difference. For thirteen years, I was employed by a certain organization, but something within me kept telling me that it was time to go. I always told myself that I wanted to be the navigator of my own destiny.

Working in human resources, I've had to coach many disgruntled employees because they decided to stay in a job for the sake of a paycheck and not fulfillment. This began to affect their performance. So, when my employer offered a buyout package, and God gave me peace, I raised my hand. Initially I thought, *Are you crazy, Sarita? You are a single mother with no husband to fall back on.* My faith was strong and I knew I had heard from God. I stepped out on faith on November 15, 2015, and left my good six-figure salary, bonus options, pension, and benefits. I went straight to the airport for a getaway trip by myself. I started writing this book, traveled more, and enjoyed time off with the girls.

After about six months, I decided it was time to get serious and start looking for employment. I applied for numerous positions I knew I was qualified for, but I received no response. Eventually I

THE QUANDARY

began to get interviews but no offers. My money started dwindling fast, but I never questioned leaving my job. I only questioned why the next door wasn't opening. What wasn't I learning? I knew passing the test was a requirement to enter the next level. I was ready to get off this roller coaster ride. It was then I started to take the process seriously. At first I relied on my savings, so I didn't have to take unemployment too seriously. I spent frivolously and enjoyed life's luxuries as if I were still working a nine-to-five job. Then, one day, unemployment ran out and my savings kept getting lower. I thought, *it's really time to buckle down and seek out additional help and network.* I was down to thirty days of savings and didn't want to tap into my retirement account.

Life has a way of presenting obstacles to get your attention. I was about to take a major plunge on my roller coaster ride. It was August 29, 2016, and I was notified that my daughter's account had been fraudulently scammed. Because I had a joint account with her, they had swiped my last bit of savings, no questions asked. That was all the money I had to my name. Instantly I had nothing. What I thought I had control of now controlled me. I couldn't pay my rent due on the first, couldn't pay my truck and credit card payments, or buy groceries. This was my rock bottom. Everything I thought was important no longer mattered. All the petty disagreements I had with people were no longer relevant. I had no plan B or anyone to enable me. I was unemployed, had no paychecks coming in, and all of my money was gone. I had two children depending on me. I felt I had nothing to offer. During uncertainty, I still had to try and keep my right mind for the girls. All I could do was cry and pray. I told the girls, "Let's pray and come into agreement for what we need." They couldn't enjoy the fruits of my experience on the mountain and not partake of the lesson in the valley.

After the first day of just crying, I said, "God, it's up to you. I have no other options." All my plans went out the door. I needed God to allow my daughters to increase their faith from this experience. I began to overthink things. Maybe if I would have done something differently, we wouldn't have been in this predicament. I'd even gotten mad at God and questioned what He was doing because, surely, He had the power to change my situation. This was another turn on the ride. I kept holding on and trusting the process of my Creator.

I began to research employers I wanted to work for. I recall seeing a position with a prestigious organization, and I wanted the Human Resources position. I prayed, tithed, and believed in God that

THE QUANDARY

it was mine. I went through the process of multiple interviews and grew more and more excited. I could finally see the end of the ride was fast approaching. I had been on this roller coaster ride for twelve months, but something within me grew in strength. It was time to get off. I was physically and emotionally tired from all the loops, turns, and bumps along the journey.

Many days I thought, *How can I be whole and complete for everyone else? I don't even know where I am or which direction this roller coaster ride is taking me. Is God hearing me when I pray? Does He see where I am and what I'm going through?* I thought surely there had to be some stored-up benefits for me as a faithful tither. It's always during the test that the teacher is silent. My spirit grew stronger to keep pressing and trusting the process. I finished the final loop when I received a call: "The job is yours." The prize was more than I had expected. I walked away from the experience with more character and a testimony. God will make a way.

God knows exactly what He is doing. Don't try to shortcut the process by helping God. That can cause the process to take longer. Do your best, but remain open to the flow of the Spirit. So many people want the benefits that trust produces but don't want to complete the process. They don't want a finished work. They want a compromise. Trust is that five letter word that means you must wait a little longer. This may be how you feel when you pray for God to change your husband's heart, heal a sick family member, or provide a financial blessing to your home. God's reply is, trust me through the process because my grace is sufficient. To trust the process means you relinquish your control to the will of God. Although you don't know the specific outcome, you know it will be for your good. Faith is the substance of things hoped for, and the evidence of things unseen.

If I didn't believe in the process of life, I couldn't have handled the death of my dad and brother. After all, God could have healed them on this side, but He chose to heal them in heaven. Going through the process isn't easy. It requires discipline and faith that what you're believing in will happen, but if it doesn't, you will accept God's will. I recall for years praying, fasting, and believing for God to deliver George. I just knew one day he would have a street ministry where he would be able to minister to other drug dealers and addicts. I believed, but learned I couldn't make him do something outside of his own will and ability. Regardless of how much you may love the other person or see him going down a path of destruction, trust the process.

The day we found out George had died; my worst fear came

THE QUANDARY

to pass. That was the conclusion of our prayers for deliverance and healing. After twenty-seven years, there were no other prayers to pray, but to ask for comfort. In just moments, there were no more words that could have been spoken for deliverance or change. What I had done ritualistically for twenty-seven years was no longer required. When something is final, it doesn't allow for more hopes or dreams. You accept there's now a period at the end of the sentence. In my mind, there was so much more that was supposed to be said or done. What was I supposed to do now with the dreams of a long life together, laughter, fussing, and raising our kids together? I had no control over life's existence. I had to trust the conclusion to the process. I had to believe my last time telling George I loved him was enough for him to know. The process didn't end the way I had wanted, but I had to have faith in God's wisdom that He knew best.

Everyone's process is very different. Maybe for you, the process is to step out on faith to apply for the job fore which you're not qualified. Maybe it's getting over the fear of starting a new relationship after being hurt. Perhaps you've been talking about starting your own catering business because everyone at the office always asks you to cook for the company potlucks. The process is designed to break down what is puffed up in your life and guide your course. When you discover yourself going through a trial, ask yourself, *What area of my life is being attacked?*

I'm a visual learner, so when I'm under attack, I perceive it as an internal infection. God needs to apply his antibiotic (deliverance) to kill the infection. When you injure yourself, exposing the scar tissue to the elements makes it easily accessible for bacteria to creep in, causing an infection of a hardened heart, a rebellious spirit, a lying tongue, or even jealousy. When you pray, God searches you to apply his antibiotic. How many of you have prayed, "Lord, search my heart, and if you find anything in me not like you, please remove it"? Watch what you ask for. That's what initiates the healing balm to your infectious areas. The healing process starts off as pain in the infected areas. This shows you where you need to pay special attention. Ignoring the symptoms and sweeping that issue under the rug makes the area more irritated. You won't go to the doctor, but instead self-diagnose in hopes the injury will go away. After a few weeks or months, the pain intensifies to the point you go running to the emergency room, better known as the church. You don't care about the cost; you just want to get rid of this pain.

The same is true when God speaks to you in your quiet time. He asks you to bless someone you know doesn't like you. You ask yourself, *Why should I? I didn't do anything to her.* Then the internal infection begins to spread into anger and resentment. Every time you see this person, you begin to feel animosity and you don't know why. After months, have gone by, you have developed bitterness and jealousy for this person. Now God must take you through the process of pruning your pride. If you would have just dealt with blessing the person when God told you in the beginning, you could have alleviated this trial.

Trusting the process sometimes means having to say no. "No" is not a curse word, nor does it imply you are mean. I know that, as an enabler, you might feel if you don't do it, who will? Get over yourself and know that the world will go on. Every assignment isn't for you to handle. When you finally muster up the strength within you to say no, you relinquish your responsibility and put the onus back on the individual to be accountable. Could it be that God created each of us to be responsible for our own decisions? Saying no without having to give an explanation is like grown-folks stuff, but this too is a process.

As I think about the life cycle of the caterpillar turning into a butterfly, I am amazed. I love butterflies, because they signify change, and I'm progressively changing into something more beautiful daily. When a butterfly is born, it's very small and attached to a tree leaf from which it can eat. It doesn't just wake up one day and fly, but it goes through an isolation period called metamorphosis. This is when the caterpillar changes its form, structure, and substance into an adult butterfly. It can't be assisted with its transformation or it will be crippled for life. It is during the isolation and struggle of breaking through the cocoon that the butterfly fully develops and transforms.

Steps to getting through the process:
- Accept it: don't resist, back up, or get mad
- Don't rush to get out of it
- Ask for wisdom
- Hold your tongue (be quick to hear and slow to speak)
- Learn the lesson

A proverb says if you give a man a fish, you will feed him for a day, but if you teach a man to fish, he will be fed for a lifetime. God expects us to be both helpful and wise. Part of that wisdom involves monitoring how we help to make sure we are not enabling. A person who is acting out self-destructively has no reason to change if they do not ever suffer consequences for their behavior. It's time to stop being surrogate parents to adults; just cut the umbilical cord once and for all. The consequences of the process may not be assigned to you, but since you're an enabler to their situation, you will go through the outcome. The outcome will consist of the pain, side effects, and symptoms as if it were your test. Stretch your faith and trust God throughout the process. When you learn the lesson, you don't have to have the same test again on a different day. The redundancy of having to take the same test is nerve-racking. The only time the teacher retains you is when the information he taught has not been learned.

Many times, as enablers, we don't allow those dysfunctional relationships to go through their process. We want to help them. We cover up their embarrassments so they won't have to deal with them. Per author Darlene Lancer, *Are You an Enabler* "It's important to leave the evidence intact, so they see how their drug use is affecting their lives. Consequently, you shouldn't clean up vomit, wash soiled linens, or move a passed-out addict into bed. This might sound cruel, but remember that the addict caused the problem. Because the addict is under the influence of an addiction, accusations, nagging, and blaming are not only futile but unkind. All theses inactions should be carried out in a matter-of-fact manner."

Identify what helps you manage the process. I love to journal because it's therapeutic and allows me to express myself without being judged. Here's my journal entry as I sat on the cruise ship on Thanksgiving 2010 as I learned my dad had just passed:

Goodbye Letter to Dad (11/23/10)

  I remember the day and hour I was told you took your last breath. I had to muster the words to say goodbye over the phone from thousands of miles away on a ship. They wouldn't wait another forty-eight hours to remove you from the ventilator, so I could be there. I didn't think I could emotionally handle it. I was thousands of miles away from land and my mind raced to and fro, and I didn't know what to do. There was no one to really comfort me, although many were around. My thoughts immediately went to how such a perfect and sovereign God could allow me the opportunity to be with you side by side through oncology appointments, chemotherapy, and family issues and not allow me to see you take your last breath. I felt I wasn't there for you at the end. You know our personalities....We don't start anything we can't finish, and I wasn't able to finish this course with you as I had planned. I know there's a bigger purpose to why things ended the way they did, but I guess I'll just have to wait until I make it to heaven to hear it. Since you've been gone, I've tried to continue to stay strong for me and the family, but I miss you terribly. I miss our daily phone calls to just say hi and coming to visit you at the Verizon Center, where you would introduce me to the same

THE QUANDARY

friends over and over just, because you were proud of me as your daughter.

Life will never be the same without you. A piece of my past is gone. On Sunday, I put up your mini-Redskins Christmas tree just to have another piece of you visible in the house. You were my strength and the one man who knew me and understood me, maybe because we were so much alike. I loved the way I always felt safe and protected with you. When we walked down the street, you never allowed me (even as an adult) to walk close to the street. You would always encourage us to leave your house before it got dark. You didn't want us driving at night. Then you called to make sure we arrived home safely. Now you are with God and have another purpose to praise and worship. My assignment isn't complete on earth, so I must press on. I will continue to share pictures of you with Imani so she will always remember you, and I will reminisce with Ebony and Kaylah about all the fun times we've shared. I finally understand the hurt, pain, and void you felt losing your parents. I love you and miss you tremendously.

Love always,

Sarita Lynn

It's time for you to trust the process. Take your time to reflect on the Action Plan questions and answer them truthfully. Your change is only as authentic as your answers.

Your Action Plan

What are you afraid to let go of?

_____
_____
_____
_____
_____
_____
_____

What will it cost you?

_____
_____
_____
_____
_____
_____
_____

THE QUANDARY

CHAPTER *Six*

When Enough Is Enough

Start moving, although you may not know where the path will lead, and the destination will become clearer. The most precious gift you can give someone is your love and time. Love is an emotion that's followed up with action. Time can never be replaced, so how you spend your time is important. You don't have time to waste doing things that will not benefit your purpose and destiny because you can't get those hours back.

Time is our most precious commodity. Everyone is given the same 24 hours in a day, so how you allocate those hours show where your priorities lie. Growing up my dad was a stickler for time, so I learned at a young age the importance of punctuality. To this day, I hate to be late for anything. I plan my day with the end in mind. I calculate when I need to be somewhere and plan backward. I anticipate how long it will take me to get dressed and arrive at my destination,

THE QUANDARY

leaving some wiggle room for traffic. I've learned everyone does not have the same priorities when it comes to her time. I admit, I take it personally when people doesn't value my time and are constantly late. Not only are they late, but when they show up, it's no big deal for them. They say, "Sarita, when I say 2:00, it really means around that time, give or take 30 minutes." This shows me that they do not value my time the way I do, so I reevaluate how much access they get from me. You can't change anyone, but you have control to whom you allocate your time.

You've given people time, love, money, rides, prayer, and even scolding, but nothing has changed them. You find yourself frustrated and angry. You started smoking, excessively drinking, and cursing, and now you've allowed their situation to negatively impact your life. This isn't even your problem. It's time for you to get up, stand in front of the mirror, and tell yourself, *Enough is enough.*

My decision for declaring "enough is enough" was probably a year or two before George passed. It was as if a light bulb went off that said, *Sarita, you can't do this anymore. You've been enabling George for twenty-seven years, and it's time for you to focus solely on raising your children. There's nothing else for you to do but pray.* This wasn't the first time I tried to stop enabling George, but this time was different. I was at the breaking point of being fed up. I was going through a divorce, I didn't qualify for a loan modification to keep my home, so I had to move out of the five-bedroom home we had built. I was now a single mom of two daughters, and I had the rest of my life to plan for. I was ready to start my new chapter.

    I had to finally allow George to be accountable for his decisions. If he was hungry I would feed him, but I wouldn't put money in his pocket. I offered him a place to sleep but with my rules. His overnight visits never lasted more than a few days. He wasn't changing, but I was, and he and my family saw it. It was a hard decision to make but harder to implement. I had enabled a dysfunctional behavior for so long it was uncomfortable to change. Initially, it did put some distance between us because I no longer had tolerance for the things I had accepted when I was twenty. I was forty-four and needed to treat George for the age he was, and not the age he wanted to act. This was difficult but I had to do it. I didn't accept his lifestyle, but I loved him and wanted the best for him. One thing about George, though—he had enough respect for his family that he wouldn't bring his lifestyle to the house.

    The process and journey doesn't always end the way we pray, but you must accept what God allows. When we finally were told by the officer that George had passed, it was numbing. We asked if we could drive to Baltimore to the Chief Medical Examiner to see the body, but we were denied. They told us they would send his body

THE QUANDARY

within two days to the funeral home of our choosing. This would be the soonest we could see him. That was the longest two days of our lives. By then, it had been four days since he had passed. Know that the decisions you make don't just impact you but those connected to you as well. Maybe your situation isn't as horrific as mine, but you still have a situation that's causing you to enable another person's destructive behavior. You're telling yourself things need to change.

"Enough is enough" isn't about just being fed up and tired. It's the anthem to yourself—it's time to do things differently. Don't stop now; complete your action plan today to hold yourself accountable to live for a purpose, and not to appease everyone's wishes of you. "Enough is enough" is demonstrated through action and without words. The culmination of your daily decisions requires others to take notice because they are seeing something different about you. It's no longer lip service, but putting action behind what you say. People may even start to think something is wrong with you because you are acting differently. That is okay. It means you are finally taking care of yourself. They've never seen this side of you. By making yourself a priority, you move out of their codependency seat. This is a season that's unfamiliar even to you. Some of the people you're used to enabling will miraculously leave your life because you're no longer meeting their needs. That's a good thing. It's time to clean house. At first making yourself a priority might feel uncomfortable, causing you to feel guilty. Because you're so used to being their go-to person for everything, you must learn a new behavior of responding. As you make the decision to change, your posture and decisions will slowly diminish their view of you as their plan B. Lead them to God. He's better equipped to handle them.

I recall a few years back, I was getting a phone call daily from a good friend constantly wanting a favor. It was always something and, because I'm a giver, he tried to take advantage of my willingness to help. After about a week, I found myself not wanting to take his calls, becoming frustrated and irritated. I thought, *I already have two kids and don't want another.* I had a decision to make. Do I value this person enough to give honest feedback or just ignore him and change my number? I decided I didn't want to be inconvenienced by changing my number, so I had to put on my big girl pants and had a heart-to-heart conversation in love. I told him I didn't mind helping occasionally but wasn't able to assist with all his needs. I was then able to connect him with local county resources that would benefit the family long-term. It's okay to instruct people to resources for help, but if you start being their problem-solver on all issues, you will not be able to stop the cycle.

Setting boundaries is crucial to any relationship. Boundaries aren't designed to keep people out of your life and living in isolation. As a matter of fact, they're designed to keep you healthy, so you can show up daily as your authentic self. Not having boundaries can deplete you by trying to be too many things to too many people. You'll be one-third of yourself, one-third who someone wants you to be, and one-third of the masks you use to cope. Oftentimes in the hustle and bustle of life, we get so busy going to work, being parents, running errands, and volunteering that we forget to take care of ourselves.

Doing anything in excess is counterproductive. We all need balance. If we don't make ourselves a priority, we could begin to display physical warning signs in our body. These signs are an alarm telling us something is out of alignment and needs adjusting. If you do not make an immediate shift, physical ailments will begin to manifest. The great thing about God is that He designed our bodies to give us indicators when something isn't operating the way He created it. He does this in hopes that we seek Him for guidance. One of the things we might need to let go of is codependency that has affected us for years, and we've allowed it to become the norm. It's now time to eradicate the issue or person from our lives. Some of these symptoms might be concealing themselves as insomnia, high blood pressure, high cholesterol, diabetes, a short temper, the inability to be without a man or woman, frustration, or enablement. These are all contrary to living your best life with purpose.

God's word says, "Seek ye first the kingdom of God and his righteousness, and all these things will be added to you. Therefore, do not be anxious about tomorrow, for tomorrow will be anxious for itself. Sufficient for the day is its own trouble" (Matthew 6:33–34). Because God loves us so and is such a gentleman, He will not force His will upon us. He waits for us to become exhausted trying to change people in our own strength and surrender. It is then He steps in to take over. I know because I've been down this road many times. As I mature, I'm learning to get by myself and truly cast my care on the One who knows me best. The process of releasing control is surrendering and allowing ourselves to be vulnerable to a higher source.

When we notice we are displaying physical warning signs, we should step back and evaluate how we are spending our time. Getting better may require seeking professional and/or spiritual guidance. God can do anything, suddenly, but He also uses counselors and doctors to treat our ailments. We have authority and control over our actions. Even if we don't feel like it, we often should make decisions contrary to how we feel for the betterment of our future. If you are anything like me, you've done enough things for the sake of just doing them. I did things just because someone else expected me to do them. Moving forward, I commit to being true to myself. I will continue to love everyone, but everything I do has to be unto pur pose. My time is precious and it can't be wasted on trivial acts. There are some things I need to start doing better, but I will be taking a lot off my plate. Forgiveness is the key to healing. Once you've forgiven yourself and have healed, it's time for you to forgive the person(s) you've enabled for years.

Ask yourself, will you believe in love again when it didn't work out the first few times? When you say "Enough is Enough," it isn't a woman's anthem to never love again. Trust that the right person will come into your life, but test and verify the validity of their actions. Don't go around with your head in the sand that you don't have common sense. Heed the warning signs. Let's say you have a standard type of guy you are attracted to. He may be a tall cup of chocolate milk about six-foot-three with a muscular build, bald head, and beard. Every time you see someone fitting this description, you look on his ring finger to see if he's married. You start wondering if you could be married to him, but you don't even know his name. Don't be so eager to have anyone in your life that you accept being mistreated and without challenging his behavior.

God always gives you adequate time to remain in a season to rest and regroup, but not enough time to delay purpose. Some people think it takes God a long time to move them through their seasons, but it doesn't. It's all conditioned on how quickly you respond to His guidance and pass the test. I can't think of anyone who likes to stay in an uncomfortable season longer than necessary. The choice is yours. Drawing your anchor and continuing your course is a decision you must make. Your decision to do the right thing quickly can cause your roller coaster ride to end sooner than someone who didn't begin.

Moving doesn't mean you know what you'll be facing down the road but you trust God. It will work out for your good. When God commanded Jonah to go to Nineveh, he didn't want to go, and decided to go in the opposite direction to Tarshish. His disobedience nearly caused those connected to Jonah to suffer the consequence of death. Disobedience not only affects you but also those around you. Disobedience has no barriers or boundaries. It spreads into other areas of your life because you're not where you're supposed to be or accomplishing your predestined assignment. Life is a journey so celebrate your successes along the way.

Take your time to reflect on the Action Plan questions and answer them truthfully. Your change is only as authentic as your answers.

THE QUANDARY

Your Action Plan

What's causing you to be fed up?

_____
_____
_____
_____
_____
_____
_____

What was your tipping point?

_____
_____
_____
_____
_____
_____
_____

Your Action Plan

When are you going to start doing what makes you happy and not feel guilty about it?

_____

_____
_____
_____
_____
_____
_____
_____
_____
_____
_____
_____
_____
_____
_____
_____

THE QUANDARY

CHAPTER *Seven*

Moving Past the Pain and Forgiving

When I seek the questions that need to be answered, I start from within. When the responses to my answers lead only to silence, I must wonder if I'm asking the right questions. To move past your pain, you first must acknowledge your anger, frustration, and disappointment, and take ownership of those feelings. Not owning up to them incarcerates you emotionally with no jail sentence. Get free by admitting you wasted valuable years trying to make someone be whom you thought he should be, but it hasn't worked. Be honest with where you are because I'm not here to judge you. Strip the resentment you have for the one you allowed to take advantage of you. This will require you to tap into the core of your positivity and find a healthy way to release it. You should make yourself vulnerable to feeling the pain, processing the effects it has on you and not cover ing it up. Reflect on the years of turmoil and mistreatment, the tears shed, and peel back the layers of abuse, betrayal, lies, cover-ups, and manipulation.

This is your sacred space to heal and not be manipulated or judged. You can no longer see yourself as the victim but must realize everything you've encountered has made you stronger. It's only then you can help free someone else. There are some situations you encounter in life that are not just for you, but for someone else. You encounter them because you're strong enough to handle it. If you weren't, the person you are assigned to strengthen might not survive it without you. You are not a victim. Playing the victim has gained you some temporary perks such as sympathy and attention from people who wouldn't ordinarily paid you any attention.

By the way, you're the strong one of the circle, so what could you possibly need? You show up when needed, and although you fuss a little, you get the job done. You chose to fill that vacancy of enabler. Unless someone held a gun to your head every day of that relationship, you've had a choice whether to stay in or terminate the position. Luckily, now it's time to resign and quit on the spot. This is the type of position for which you don't have to put in a two-week notice to your employer. This is an at-will position, which means you can quit on the spot with no notice. Don't worry; you will not be needing them as a reference to fill a similar role. There's always a choice and consequences with our decisions.

Now that we've accepted that we aren't victims, we can face our own reality. Keep in mind, there's a blessing at the end of the pain, and we can forgive. Pain is never fun but necessary for healing and breakthrough. I've been told that I'm sensitive, and that surprised me the first time I heard it. My entire life, I've always had this invisible fortress around me that prevented me from being too emotional. I felt that being too sensitive was a sign of weakness. I'm a nurturer at heart until I feel I'm being taken advantage of. Then I'm done. But it takes a lot for me to get to that point. I would forgive and go right back to the same enabling behavior. I remember times when Felicia and I were younger and we would come together to pray. She would start getting emotional and cry. I would think, *Oh, Lord, really... this is spiritual warfare, so why are you crying? We're going into battle and there's no time for this emotional stuff. Let's fight.* I was so insensitive. Going through enough humbling situations in the past six years has caused me to be more sensitive and empathetic. It has produced compassion and understanding in me. I want to see everyone blessed and not to judge anyone because I'm far from perfect. I take a person at their word, and that's become a rare commodity for my generation these days. No one says what he means or means what he says. It's just words. So when you can get to the place where you can be real with who you are, which is not a victim, and accept the totality of your life experiences, you can forgive yourself and your offender.

For women, giving birth is a painful process, but at the end, you hope to receive a beautiful, healthy baby. I remember when I gave birth to my oldest daughter, Ebony, and the overwhelming feeling of love I had toward her. I never thought I could love another person so unconditionally. I had dated and was married to her dad, but it was different when I gave birth. That last push of pain produced an everlasting love. After carrying her for nine months and gaining fifty-seven pounds, and with her weighing 9 pounds 9.6 ounces, I loved her despite the pain I endured of the delivery. It was no longer about me or what I wanted. All the pain and discomfort I went through being pregnant for nine months went out the door after that final push, and I received my blessing.

Many of you are going through a birthing process right now and are frustrated because of the morning sickness of the kids not acting right. You can't sleep through the night because the job is getting on your nerves. Your feet are swelling because you're tired of beating the pavement looking for another job to make ends meet. Anything we give birth to comes from a process. The process can be uncomfortable, inconvenient, and sometimes take longer than what we think it should, but trust God.

God's timing is perfect. The sooner we take our hands off the situation, sometimes repent, and ask God what we need to do to learn, the sooner we progress in our trimesters. A pregnancy has three trimesters. The first three months is trimester one when the fetus/God's seed has been deposited for purpose. Your purpose is beginning to receive the nutrients of your faith to grow. In the beginning, it's going to be hard and uncomfortable because of the life changes you're going through. You will begin to be tired and sluggish from all the other commitments, but keep it moving. If you do not provide your seed with daily affirmations, encouragement, and prenatal prayer, you can easily miscarry because the enemy is coming to steal, kill, and destroy, but God has come to give you life more abundantly. *Your prayers defeat the words of a foolish heart.*

In your second trimester, weeks fourteen to twenty-eight, your purpose is beginning to outgrow the confinements of the space you have, and you begin to get irritated and tell God you're ready for a change now. What's taking so long for my blessing to come? You're ready to leave your job, get married, get divorced, buy the house, or leave the church. We serve a perfect God and He will not allow you to deliver now because your purpose will be premature with the possibility of miscarriage or birth defects. Wow, how many times have we tried to rush God for a season in our lives when He just wants us to wait a little while longer for the full, mature, developed blessing? Love conquers all.

Because you were obedient and didn't abort purpose and destiny, you have made it to your last trimester. The book is finished. You've applied for the job. You've lost twenty pounds. Many of you are there now, and you've endured. You prayed, fasted, wrote the business plan, networked, saved your money, got healed, and it's about to pay off, if you just hold on another few weeks. Your baby is fully formed, and your blessing is about to come forth. When I pushed that last push and Ebony was delivered through the birthing canal, the doctor asked, "Who will cut the umbilical cord?" Many of you as adults have relationships to which you should cut the umbilical cord. It's time for them to obtain their nutrients from another source. 1 Peter 5:10 says, "And after you have suffered a little while, the God of all grace, who has called you to his eternal glory in Christ, will himself restore, confirm, strengthen and establish you." I don't know about you, but it's my season of being established. All we have gone through is in the name of love.

Sometimes moving past the pain doesn't lend itself to a positive outcome. Maybe the person might not be healed from cancer on this side, your family member might get time in jail, or your child won't get accepted into college, but how are you going to handle it? To move past the pain, a reality check is needed, and maybe you need to realize the person with whom you are angry is dealing with a disease they cannot control. It may be beyond your ability to help them. It took me a long time to face the fact that drug addiction is a disease and not everyone can break it, even with professional help. I used to get so mad at George for not being strong enough to break his addiction. I blamed him for not fighting harder. I know he wanted to be drug free, but he didn't know how. He went through drug rehabilitation, jail, and counseling, but the struggle was real. I wanted so badly for him to just wake up one morning and be drug free. The inner struggles and pain were too much for him.

You see, people don't get high or intoxicated, gamble, or steal just for the sake of it. Most of the time, they are masking an inward pain they don't want to or know how to deal with. George was masking many pains. One was never having a close relationship with my dad, so he turned to the streets for masculine validation. George had nurturing and enabling at home but didn't have a male role model when he most needed one. In turn, he acted out.

I had to learn to look at George through new lenses of grace because of the grace of God, that could have been me. As a teenager, I also tried getting high, drinking, being sexually active, and so forth, but I didn't become addicted to any. I wasn't an alcoholic, although I was surrounded by them. I went through a period of guilt asking God why George got hooked and not me. I'm grateful God kept me during my immature decisions. I could no longer look down on George, but had to have compassion and forgive him. I not only had to forgive him for participating in activities that ended his life too soon, but I had to forgive myself for enabling him for twenty-seven years. That took so much out of me. Sometimes I feel my life experiences have aged me beyond my forty-eight years on earth. I have a very low tolerance for a lot of nonsense.

When my dad was diagnosed with colon cancer in 2009, I was at every oncology appointment. I was his part-time caregiver, changed his ostomy bag, and showed up to the emergency room during the middle of the night if he got sick, among other things. While

MOVING PAST THE PAIN AND FORGIVING

I was on my cruise there were decisions made not to wait another 48-hours for my return to remove my dad from his breathing tube. I didn't agree with that decision, but I had to forgive and let go of the pain. If I didn't I would live with hatred and animosity toward others, so I forgave. Today, I stand stronger and better for the trials I've gone through.

Make a shift. Letting go of your pain is giving yourself permission to let your guard down. Being vulnerable requires shedding of self and being exposed to others. Having your guard up can be a learned behavior. People have gotten so accustomed to entering relationships and saying my guard is up as if it's become the norm. Having your guard up isn't so much about being a victim as it is about needing to be in control. Relationships are meant to be enjoyed and not be violent. A boxer makes a living fighting and going on the attack to conquer their opponent all twelve rounds. It's a combat sport in which two people throw punches at each other in hopes of knocking down their opponent, while defending themselves.

Entering relationships with partners who admit to having their guards up should send you for the hills running. This shows they are emotionally unavailable to give you all of themselves in a relationship. They are always seeking validation and approval and still have unresolved issues with something from their past.

If relationships were not supposed to be hurtful, then why was I always saying my guard was up every time I entered a new relationship? I didn't want to get hurt. The words I was speaking were preparing me for disappointment. I went into the relationship on the defensive and wondered why it didn't work.

You shouldn't have to have an exit plan or defend yourself from the people who say they love you. So why is your guard up? Let your guard down because we're being called into vulnerability and freedom. When your guard is up, you are covering your face, which prevents you from properly seeing. It will be totally up to you, if you have the time to invest in their deliverance, which might or might not happen.

Thinking about this made me really step back and rethink how I'd been confronting my relationships, and what I needed to do to change. I was attracting unavailable men, which perpetuated my hurt. Broken people attract other broken people. I attracted what I knew. I linked up with men who looked good on the outside but were emotionally unavailable. When I walked out the door I had my masks on to cover up the pain I was feeling. I wasn't fooling anyone but myself. A person who is truly confident and intuitive can detect an imitator a mile away. I sure can now.

It's amazing how some people stereotype others based on generalizations and assumptions about an individual or a group of people. These generalizations can be positive or negative. Some people are under the belief that all skinny people are healthy and all overweight people are unhealthy. I know plenty of thin people who are unhealthy eaters and never exercise with high blood pressure. Looks can be deceiving; they just have a fast metabolism but are still unhealthy. Generalizations can be as deep as assuming all black people can play basketball or all Asians are good in math. Stop assuming and get to know each other as individuals.

Life can guide you down a path you never thought you'd be on. You're confronted with circumstances you wish you could have avoided but couldn't. Sometimes when you find yourself in heartache, ask yourself, *Am I resisting the shift? Am I not going with the natural flow life is trying to take me in?* This will cause your soul to be in direct opposition with your spirit. Your soul wants to have its way. Your soul comprises of your mind, will, and emotions. It's only when you take your hands off and say, "Yes, Lord," that the natural flow of your spirit will move forward.

We should bring positivity to the words we speak about

ourselves and others. We were not created to be suspicious that everyone is out to get us. That's the learned behavior of paranoia. Stop speaking division and thinking everyone doesn't like you or is jealous of you because that's not the case. The truth is they probably don't care either way. Step back and look at your environment, and it will always show what you've been perpetually speaking. If you see people constantly leaving, think about how you've treated them. People are hurt and broken, and we are called to be life-givers and help support others but not enable them. Can you love someone through their decisions when you know it's not what's best? Resist feeling responsible for what's not yours.

Tears heal; the cleansing is therapeutic for you. Tears make you come to the truth of who you are or what you've told yourself about you or your situation.

Take your time to reflect on the Action Plan questions and answer them truthfully. Your change is only as authentic as your answers.

Your Action Plan

What pain are you suppressing that's holding you bound?

_____

_____

_____

_____

_____

_____

_____

_____

Who do you need to forgive?

_____

_____

_____

_____

_____

_____

_____

ТHE QUANDARY

CHAPTER *Eight*
Making Me a Priority

The journey inward takes a concerted effort to look at the person in the mirror in order to live your dreams. You can no longer avoid all of the imperfections of your decisions that have left you with remnants of blemishes and scars. Although the scars have healed, they are there as a reminder of what you've been through and overcome. This is the time to be selfish and live for yourself. You've taken care of the neighbor, your mother, father, sister, and brother, and now the caregiver needs caring.

When you're traveling, right before takeoff, the friendly airline stewards line up and down the aisle to review the emergency procedures. In case of an emergency, a mask will drop from a container in the airplane ceiling. You are instructed to put on your mask before helping anyone sitting with you. The mask, which looks like

THE QUANDARY

a yellow plastic cup, fits over your nose and mouth. An elastic strap goes around the back of your head and can be tightened by pulling the string. Pull on the hose gently to begin the flow of oxygen. As a mother, when I first heard the instructions, I was shocked. You're telling me to take care of myself before I can take care of my children? I had never heard that before and was alarmed. As a mom, my instinct was to be a protector and provider for my little ones. This caused me to reconsider my entire thought process. Maybe I had it wrong all along. It's okay to make sure I'm good and make myself a priority. This doesn't discount my love for Ebony or Imani. I'm not supposed to be ashamed of what others think about it. If I continue to give out and put others first, I will not be any good for me or them. This began the shift.

Growing up, I always had a direct personality. I said what I thought so no one would have to guess. That got me in a lot of trouble. Staying positive and keeping your head in the game is a choice. It requires you to be focused and determined to reach your goals regardless of distractions. Being mature means knowing every battle isn't yours. You can't carry the weight for everyone. If you keep making decisions from your emotions, you will be tossed to and fro. Be clear where you are going and what you're supposed to do. There will be hindrances, but they can only derail the assignment if you allow them. Emotions have a purpose but they're not supposed to be your sole decision factor. When what you want doesn't want you, let it go. Center in and come in accord with whom the Creator designed you to be, not you and Sally, Tiffany, or Bob.

Before the hurts and disappointments derailed your dreams, you were heading on a course. Your aim was on point, and it's time to get back to focusing on the bulls eye of your dreams. Your purpose is unique and designed just for you. What is that thing that wakes you up at three a.m. and gets you excited, but you're too afraid to do it? Yeah, that's it!

Pastor Antonio M. Matthews would always say, "Your vision should always be bigger than your budget. If it isn't, you wouldn't need God." Your destiny is too important to give up for anything or anybody. The path has been set. Relax and trust God to reveal it to you. Allow the child in you to imagine again without restrictions. Don't try to figure out everything today; just take one step at a time. You can't die full of purpose. When you finally take your last breath, you should be empty of purpose and leave a legacy. Take a deep breath and operate your faith.

Making yourself a priority may require you to put up some

parameters in your life. Being too vulnerable is a fragile state. Be careful of the information and access you give to others. Protect your heart from someone who just wants to use you. Everyone can't handle your most intimate secrets. Be true to yourself and your feelings or you never can be true to anyone else. It's time to awaken the planning of your new life. For so many years, I chose to help everyone else, and forgot about myself. No more; it's my turn. It's time to walk in our new identity. Your change can be as easy as starting that new business, refusing to give your children everything they ask for, or just holding your peace and not saying a word. Change doesn't always have to be big, but it must make a difference.

Have you ever woken and thought, *I need something in my life to change?* I had this same epiphany when George died and (he was now added to the statistics of another person dying of a drug overdose). It had nothing to do with his skin color, age, gender or ethnicity, but everything to do with having this addictive disease to which so many have succumbed. At the time, I couldn't think of how to change my situation or remove the hurt I was feeling. I thought, *I'm going to change what I look like*, and I started with my physical appearance. I know to some people this is minor, but to me I just wanted to disappear and hide. I was ashamed and embarrassed to tell people my brother had died from a drug overdose. I hadn't ac cepted the reality myself, so how could I expect anyone else? I wasn't ready to answer the questions when, where, or how. The weave allowed me to become someone else in my mind. I was desperate for change. What I thought was a cover-up was now something I loved. I loved the look so much, I gave myself an alter ego. This became fun. I could role-play depending on the day. As soon as I looked in the mirror, I said, "Hello, Tiffany." Now, how funny is that... *Who is Tiffany?* I thought. I was no longer using my new look as a mask, but to enjoy life and come outside my shell in a small way. One evening when I got home, I decided to journal about my day. While I was journaling, my spirit told me to look up the name Tiffany. I immediately thought, *Oh, gosh, what have I done now?* I went to the Internet and researched the name Tiffany. To my surprise, it means the "appearance or manifestation of God." I thought, *Wow, what I thought was my alter ego was truly a revelation of who I am, even while changing.*

    There is greatness within your reach. Don't sell yourself short because you are worth the investment. There is nothing you've gone through that can prevent you from achieving your blessings. The only thing that can derail your purpose is you. Reach for the stars. You receive only one life so live it to the fullest. Tomorrow is not promised so allow your decisions today to put you in position for greatness to morrow.

What are you going to do with your remaining days on earth? Write your plan and work it. There could be an entrepreneur in you waiting to be developed. Stay focused and concentrate on what makes you truly happy. What puts a smile on your face is nine times out of ten your passion. It's easier to pursue what comes naturally to you than something forced that merely pays the bills. This is your year to move forward. Dust off those old sketches you have tucked away in the garage and start drawing again. Start a mentoring program where you can utilize your gifts to enhance someone else's skills. Maybe you've been wanting to go back to school to finish your degree; go register. It's not too late. You're never too old to invest in your education and development. You can do this.

Keep in mind, every dream isn't meant to be shared prematurely. Some dreams should be kept in your own personal incubator until developed. Everyone you know doesn't have your best interest at heart, so protect your dream seeds from the vultures. Go start your book and tell your story. I know it can be intimidating and requires you to become vulnerable and it takes a lot of work and dedication, but think of all the people you will help. Your testimony can prevent someone from making the same mistakes you made.

Begin to speak daily affirmations over your day. Here are a few that I say:

- I possess the qualities needed to be successful
- My marriage is solid and loving, and we have great communication
- I am in good health
- I walk in power, love, and sound mind
- All my needs are met according to His riches in glory
- I forgive those who have harmed me, and I hold no grudges
- I shall have seven sources of income and be relevant and influential in all markets
- My future spouse is currently preparing himself for me, and we will be a perfect match
- I am quick to hear and slow to speak
- I make wise decisions
- I will make better decisions today than I did yesterday

Take your time to reflect on the Action Plan questions and answer them truthfully. Your change is only as authentic as your answers.

THE QUANDARY

Your Action Plan

Write two things you can accomplish in the next thirty days to make yourself a priority:

_____

_____

_____

_____

_____

_____

_____

Write two long-term goals you have been afraid to accomplish for yourself. Write the action plan:

_____

_____

_____

_____

_____

_____

_____

Conclusion

Congratulations on investing in your freedom to no longer be an enabler. I hope this book has helped you to identify the warning signs of being an enabler, and to gain the confidence to make different decisions. While completing your action plan, know it is a process. You didn't become an enabler overnight, and it may take time to completely be free. Be open to counselling and speaking with a professional, if needed. This disease is a day-by-day journey. Some days you do better than others, but make progress and don't allow others to put you in a box of guilt. You are free and don't be afraid to reflect on the experiences you've encountered because they were designed to strengthen your faith. Trust God and the plan He has for your life. Everyone's journey is as unique as fingerprints. No two are alike.

The word of God says you owe no man anything, but to love him. Love those to whom you are connected, and pray for them through their decisions. The Quandary is over…you should no longer feel responsible for what's not yours.

INTERCESSION FOR RESULTS

Prayer for *Deliverance from Enabling*

Dear Lord God, I come in the name of Jesus to thank you for allowing me to see another day. I thank you for keeping your hand on my life when I was making foolish decisions. God, I ask you to teach me to love myself how you love me. Help me to see myself as you see me. Teach me to fully accept myself so that I don't have to enable others for their acceptance and approval. Heal me from the inside out. I'm good at masking my insecurities, but help me to finally remove the mask and every pretense. Lord, I know you are able.

Heal me from the guilt I carry for all the wasted years I enabled others. Help me to forgive myself. Show me how to have healthy relationships and set realistic boundaries. I desire to love and be loved without having my guard up. Your word says you did not give me the spirit of fear but power, love, and sound mind.

I speak to my destiny that my latter days will be better than my former. Everything I stand in need of is met. In the name of Jesus.

Prayer for *Healing*

Dear Heavenly Father, I come in the name of Jesus to first say thank you for allowing me to be able to boldly come in your presence. Thank you for inclining your ear to my voice. You are such a wonderful God. I come into agreement with Isaiah 53:3: "He was wounded for our transgressions, *he was* bruised for our iniquities: the chastisement of our peace *was* upon him; and with his stripes we are healed."

I know your word is true and you care for me. You are Jehovah Rapha—the God who heals. Goodness and mercy shall follow me all the days of my life.

I come to you today asking you to heal my body from _____ (*be specific*). I ask you to remove anything that has invaded my body that is not designed to make me be in good health and to prosper as my soul prospers. I ask that you deal with the root cause of my situation and heal suddenly. I thank you that you are bringing every organ, cell, and blood issue into alignment with wholeness and healing me in the name of Jesus. Amen.

Prayer for *Prosperity*

Thank you, Lord, for what you have done in my life. I believe every decision I make is positioning me for financial wealth. Your word said in Malachi 3:10–11, "Bring ye all the tithes into the storehouse, that there may be meat in mine house, and prove me now herewith, saith the LORD of hosts, if I will not open you the windows of heaven, and pour you out a blessing, that *there shall* not *be room enough to receive it*. And I will rebuke the devourer for your sakes, and he shall not destroy the fruits of your ground; neither shall your vine cast her fruit before the time in the field, saith the LORD of hosts."

I am your child and bring back your word to your remembrance. I trust you to fulfill your promises. You are a generous God. I give thanks for giving me ideas and creativity that bring forth prosperity to this land.

Thank you for the Holy Spirit that lives within me and guides me into all wisdom. I walk in financial liberty that I can leave an inheritance to my children and my children's children. In the name of Jesus. Amen.

Prayer for *Strongholds* to Be *Broken*

Heavenly Father, I pray you will identify to me every stranglehold that is secretly lying dormant in my life. I command every demon to be eradicated from my life and the life of my family. I thank you, Lord, for your strength and courage to persevere through this fight. I know you are with me and you will never leave me nor forsake me. I pray that I would be strong in the day of battle. Your word in Psalms 37:1–2 says, "Fret not thyself because of evildoers, neither be thou envious against the workers of iniquity. For they shall soon be cut down like the grass, and wither as the green herb."

I pray that you would annihilate every stronghold of fear, doubt, insecurity, shame, or unbelief that hinders my spiritual walk. Help me to resist the devil, and he will flee. I trust you and know you are with me, for you have not given me the spirit of fear and timidity, but of power, love, self-discipline, and a sound mind. Lord, you told us to stand and put on the Whole Armor of God in the time of battle. I have my loins girt about with truth, the breastplate of righteousness, my feet shod with preparation of the gospel of peace, shield of faith, helmet of salvation, and sword of the spirit, which is the word of God. In the name of Jesus. Amen.

Prayer for *Guidance*

Lord, you promised that when I seek you with all our heart, I will find you. I seek only after you. Bring peace to my worried heart. Calm my wayward mind. I trust in only you. I've tried everything I know to do and need you to intervene on my behalf. I know I should have come sooner, but I've come to the end of myself. I need you to work this situation _____ (*be specific*) out for my good. I know your word is a lamp unto my feet and a light unto my path, and I ask you to lead me. Remove those things or people that trouble me. If you don't, give me the strength to outlast them. I release them all to you.

I know my steps are ordered by the Lord, and I trust you to get me where I'm supposed to go. It is as important for you that I'm in my right assignment so I can fulfill purpose. Remove all my fears that hinder me from movement and progress. I have courage to overcome what is trying to overcome me. This valley experience will pass, and I will be on the mountaintop soon in victory. In the name of Jesus. Amen.

Prayer for *Peace*

Dear Heavenly Father, I come in the name of Jesus to say thank you. I thank you that in the presence of the Lord is liberty. Lord Jesus, I ask you to fill me with the peace that surpasses all my understanding. I ask you to heal and deliver me from everything that is causing stress and pain in my life.

I pray you will contend with those who contend with me. Bring peace to my mind. Your word says in Romans 12:1–2, "*I beseech you therefore, brethren, by the mercies of God, that ye present your bodies a living sacrifice, holy, acceptable unto God, which is your reasonable service. And be not conformed to this world: but be ye transformed by the renewing of your mind, that ye may prove what is that good, and acceptable, and perfect, will of God.*

I pray you will make my enemies be at peace with me. Steady my soul. Raise me above my situation so I won't respond out of emotions. Allow me to soar through this storm so I can pass this test the first time. In the name of Jesus. Amen.

TAKE IT TO THE WORD

SCRIPTURAL SUPPORT

Psalms 118:5 – I called upon the LORD in distress: the LORD answered me, [and set me] in a large place.

Galatians 5:13 – For, brethren, ye have been called unto liberty; only [use] not liberty for an occasion to the flesh, but by love serve one another.

John 8:31-36 – Then said Jesus to those Jews which believed on him, If ye continue in my word, [then] are ye my disciples indeed.

Romans 6:18 – Being then made free from sin, ye became the servants of righteousness.

Romans 6:7 – For he that is dead is freed from sin.

Psalms 55:22 – Cast thy burden upon the LORD, and he shall sustain thee: he shall never suffer the righteous to be moved.

SCRIPTURAL SUPPORT, CONT'D

Acts 26:18 – To open their eyes, [and] to turn [them] from darkness to light, and [from] the power of Satan unto God, that they may receive forgiveness of sins, and inheritance among them which are sanctified by faith that is in me.

Ephesians 2:8–9 – For by grace are ye saved through faith; and that not of yourselves: [it is] the gift of God.

Acts 13:38–39 – Be it known unto you therefore, men [and] brethren, that through this man is preached unto you the forgiveness of sins.

2 Thessalonians 3:10–15 – For even when we were with you, this we commanded you, that if any would not work, neither should he eat.

SCRIPTURAL SUPPORT, CONT'D

Ephesians 5:11 – And have no fellowship with the unfruitful works of darkness, but rather reprove [them].

Proverbs 10:4 – He becometh poor that dealeth [with] a slack hand: but the hand of the diligent maketh rich.

James 4:6 – But he giveth more grace. Wherefore he saith, God resisteth the proud, but giveth grace unto the humble.

2 John 1:11 – For he that biddeth him God speed is partaker of his evil deeds.

John 14:27 – Peace I leave with you, my peace I give unto you: not as the world giveth, give I unto you. Let not your heart be troubled, neither let it be afraid.

Matthew 7:7 – Ask, and it shall be given you; seek, and ye shall find; knock, and it shall be opened unto you.

SCRIPTURAL SUPPORT, CONT'D

Philippians 4:6–7 – Be careful for nothing; but in everything by prayer and supplication with thanksgiving let your requests be made known unto God.

John 16:33 – These things I have spoken unto you, that in me ye might have peace. In the world ye shall have tribulation: but be of good cheer; I have overcome the world.

Isaiah 26:3 – Thou wilt keep [him] in perfect peace, [whose] mind [is] stayed [on thee]: because he trusteth in thee.

Romans 16:20 – And the God of peace shall bruise Satan under your feet shortly. The grace of our Lord Jesus Christ [be] with you.

Romans 8:6 – For to be carnally minded [is] death; but to be spiritually minded [is] life and peace.

SCRIPTURAL SUPPORT, CONT'D

Romans 15:13 – Now the God of hope fill you with all joy and peace in believing, that ye may abound in hope, through the power of the Holy Ghost.

Romans 5:1 – Therefore being justified by faith, we have peace with God through our Lord Jesus Christ.

Isaiah 41:10 – Fear thou not; for I [am] with thee: be not dismayed; for I [am] thy God: I will strengthen thee; yea, I will help thee; yea, I will uphold thee with the right hand of my righteousness.

Hebrews 12:14 – Follow peace with all [men], and holiness, without which no man shall see the Lord.

Luke 2:14 – Glory to God in the highest, and on earth peace, good will toward men.

LIST OF RESOURCES

Addiction Search
(800) 807-0951
http://www.addictionsearch.com/

Best Drug Rehabilitation Inc.
Drug and Alcohol Addiction Treatment Center
300 Care Center Drive
Manistee, MI 49660
1(844) 215-0638
www.bestdrugrehabilitation.com

Co-Dependents Anonymous International
PO Box 33577
Phoenix, AZ 85067-3577
(888) 444-2359 (Toll Free)
(888) 444-2379 (Spanish Toll Free)
http://coda.org/

Darlene Lancer, MA, MFT, JD
info@darlenelancer.com
http://darlenelancer.com/

LIST OF RESOURCES, CONT'D

Karen Allen
Licensed Clinical Professional Counselor (LCPC), Independent Contractor
(301) 332-7573
Karenallen600@gmail.com

Pastor Antonio M. Matthews
Tabernacle of Praise Church
3280 Leonardtown Road
Waldorf, MD 20602
www.meetmeatthetop.org
pastor@meetmeatthetop.org

PsychCentral
Symptoms of codependency:
http://psychcentral.com/lib/symptoms-of-codependency/

Tressa "Azarel" Smallwood and Tiphani Montgomery
http://www.thebestsellersproject.com/
An online program for people who want to successfully self-publish a book.

ABOUT THE AUTHOR

Sarita Lynn is the CEO of *Skie Publishing, LLC*. She has her bachelor's degree in Behavioral Social Sciences from the University of Maryland University College. Sarita currently serves on the Charles County Commission for Women Board and on the Tabernacle of Praise Church Leadership Team and Board of Advisors. She is the proud mother of two beautiful daughters, Ebony and Imani. She considers Kaylah as her third daughter. During her spare time, she enjoys traveling, journaling, volunteerism, praying, and spending time with family and close friends. It has been Sarita's faith and active prayer life that have strengthened her through life's situations.

Sarita's commitment to family is unmeasurable. Her foundational scripture is Philippians 4:6–7: "Do not be anxious about anything, but in every situation, by prayer and petition, with thanksgiving, present your requests to God. And the peace of God, which transcends all understanding, will guard your hearts and your minds in Christ Jesus."

THANK YOU

• A special thanks to my mother, Sandra Turner, and my sister Felicia Wallace, for allowing me to share our story. I know it wasn't easy to relive our experience, and share it with the world. I believe it will bless someone. Love you much.

• A huge hug and kiss to my daughters, Ebony and Imani, for giving me the freedom to focus on writing and publishing this book. I couldn't have done it without your encouragement and high expectations of me. I love you with all my heart. Kaylah, regardless of the geographical distance you will always be aunties baby.

• A special thanks to James Lambert for always encouraging me to not give up, and accepting me for who I am, and not for what I've been through. I appreciate and love you.

• Thank you, Pastor Antonio M. Matthews, for seeing my potential and always pushing me toward excellence. I truly appreciate you writing the foreword in my book. We are truly living under an open heaven.